Open for Debate

Civil
Liberties

Open for Debate

Civil Liberties

Ray Spangenburg and Kit Moser

Marshall Cavendish
Benchmark
New York

Marshall Cavendish Benchmark
99 White Plains Road
Tarrytown, NY 10591-9001
www.marshallcavendish.us

All Internet sites were available and accurate when sent to press.

Library of Congress Cataloging-in-Publication Data
Spangenburg, Ray, 1939-
Civil liberties / by Ray Spangenburg and Kit Moser.
p. cm. — (Open for debate)
Includes bibliographical references and index.
ISBN 0-7614-1886-5
1. Civil rights—United States—Juvenile literature. I. Moser, Diane,
1944- II. Title. III. Series.
JC599.U5S5996 2005
323'.0973—dc22
2005001165

Photo research by Linda Sykes Picture Research, Inc., Hilton Head, SC

Series design by Sonia Chaghatzbanian

Printed in China
1 3 5 6 4 2

Contents

THE TWIN TOWERS OF THE WORLD TRADE CENTER IN NEW YORK CITY BURST INTO FLAME ON SEPTEMBER 1, 2001, WHEN HIJACKERS PILOTED TWO COMMERCIAL JET AIRLINERS ON A COLLISION COURSE WITH THE EXTREMELY HIGH STRUCTURES. THE ATTACKS CHANGED MANY AMERICANS' ATTITUDES ABOUT THE SECURITY OF THEIR NATION.

Foreword

Growing up in the United States of America, most members of this country's varied populace are proud to call their home the "land of the free." For those who have come recently to American shores, part of the attraction was this characteristic of life in America.

At the same time, freedom can exact a steep price. Allowing everyone freedom can involve grave risks. Before September 11, 2001, a small group of people from other countries were issued visas and allowed to enter the United States. Here, they learned how to pilot jets, obtained passenger tickets, and—on the day that will forever be known as 9/11—gained entry as passengers on four jetliners transporting innocent citizens. They proceeded to hijack the planes they had boarded and turned them into weapons. A horrified nation watched the terror reenacted on videotape as the jets crashed into two World Trade Center buildings and the Pentagon, which were filled with unsuspecting workers. Thousands were killed. Later, many people asked why these nineteen individuals, secretly determined to become martyrs, were allowed into the country; why American training schools trained the pilots; why they all had the freedom to come and go as they needed; and why authorities did not prevent their collaboration, notice their plan for this tragic scenario, or finally keep them from boarding those planes.

After 9/11, many details came to light, some of which were known to a few government agencies before the strike. The terrorists turned out to be part of a terrorist group called al Qaeda, run by Osama bin Laden, who was thought to be working from Afghanistan and has master-minded many other terrorist attacks worldwide. Their actions were suspicious enough to have raised questions. Why had the government not acted to prevent the strikes, if prior knowledge was available? Was it a case of too much freedom given too liberally? Or was it a case of ineffectual use of available information?

These questions are not confined to the events of 9/11. These kinds of questions come up every day in law enforcement, in the courts, in public schools—wherever government touches the everyday lives of people. And in a post-9/11 world, they have become ever more urgent. Unlike many other countries, Americans have rarely experienced the fear of foreign attacks on American soil. Now the homeland was threatened. Americans came to know terror in their hearts. A new agency, the Department of Homeland Security, was formed. Congress enacted broad new laws. The American government went about making America safer for Americans. Airline passengers now had to pass more intrusive baggage inspections and personal searches before entering secured areas of airports and before boarding airplanes. Some people began to talk about the need for a national identity card for everyone residing in the United States. Agencies such as the Federal Bureau of Investigation (FBI) began to increase surveillance. Hundreds of people were arrested and detained without explanation. Procedures described as torture were used on prisoners suspected of terrorist affiliations. Demands for racial profiling in law enforcement became more prevalent and more urgently voiced.

These measures grew out of the most understandable concerns. Home should be a safe place to live and raise children. It should provide a sanctuary where one's defenses do not have to be constantly up. It should be a place where one can feel safe from harm, physically, emotionally, and mentally. Now we are on alert. Osama bin Laden's Egyptian deputy, Ayman al-Zawahiri, spoke on an audiotape aired in October 2004, in which he called on young members of al Qaeda and others "to strike the United States and its allies." Americans now know that without vigilance tragedy can again affect their daily lives and well-being.

But what if these important interests—safety and liberty—come into conflict, as they often do? How do we resolve that conflict? Many observers wonder how many essential American liberties may be lost in the process of protecting ourselves against terrorism and crime.

Civil liberties function as a check on the power of government. They safeguard the lives, property, privacy, and freedoms of individuals against encroachment by the state. What if we trade in too much of our liberty for security? Caught on the horns of dilemma, we know that we may lose our lives, our livelihood, and the health of our economy if we do not find ways to protect ourselves better than we did before 9/11. And yet, if in protecting ourselves we lose the great freedoms that form the basis for American life, what will we have left?

How can we find a balance that serves both these needs? This is one of the most pressing questions of our time.

This book introduces issues inherent in this controversial topic and the pros and cons—the pluses and minuses—of the major choices currently faced by the branches of government and the people for whom it exists.

1
Civil Liberties and 9/11

The tragedy of September 11, 2001, is several years in the past. Yet its legacy is still very much with us. The circumstances were extraordinary. The future looked fearsome. And strong action was unquestionably required. In the hours following the airline crashes and toppling buildings, President George W. Bush's location was undisclosed, and Vice President Dick Cheney secretly went to a separate emergency location to protect the continuity of the government in the event of further attacks. All air traffic in the skies above the United States was grounded. People traveling on business trips were stranded, sometimes thousands of miles from their homes and families. No one was sure what would happen in the days to come.

Over the days, weeks, and months that followed, President Bush, his cabinet, and the U.S. Congress took many measures designed to prevent future attacks and to punish those who contributed to terrorism against the United States.

Extensive airport baggage and personal searches were stepped up. Individuals suspected of terrorist connections were rounded up and imprisoned. Troops were marshaled to search for the terrorist leader Osama bin Laden and to unseat the Taliban government in Afghanistan, which had given sanctuary to bin Laden and the terrorist enclaves of al Qaeda. A new law known as the USA PATRIOT Act broadened the investigative powers of government agents such as police officers and Federal Bureau of Investigation (FBI) agents. (Its name is an acronym standing for Uniting and Strengthening America by Providing Appropriate Tools Required to Intercept and Obstruct Terrorism.)

As the efforts to stave off future terrorist attacks built up, some observers became concerned about losses of liberty, a treasured and fundamental feature of American life for which U.S. citizens have fought many times since the Declaration of Independence was signed in 1776.

Civil Liberties in Time of National Emergency

Early in the days following September 11, 2001, and frequently thereafter, President George W. Bush expressed his intention to try high-ranking terrorist suspects secretly, in military courts, outside the public court system. That statement began a highly contested policy that many people thought was ill-advised and unconstitutional. One prisoner, José Padilla, a U.S. citizen, was arrested in 2002 as an operative of al Qaeda thought to be planning to explode a low-grade nuclear bomb. He was declared an enemy combatant and held incommunicado except for his lawyers. A request by his lawyers for Supreme Court review of his case was refused in June 2004 on technical grounds. Not until February 2005 did a federal district court in South Carolina rule that the government could not hold Padilla indefinitely without access to a court, with a directive to charge or release him. Still, as of the end of June 2005, Padilla remains in prison, with a Supreme Court decision asserting that Padilla's case was brought to the wrong court.

However, Bush is not the first president to take extraordinary measures in time of national emergency, and he did have reasons. In a December 2001 hearing before the U.S. Senate Judiciary Committee, Attorney General John Ashcroft explained that the military court was a more appropriate venue for trying terrorist cases than the open public court for two reasons. First, much classified material was likely to come out in such a trial and should not, for the security of the nation, be aired in public. Second, the safety of all persons involved in such a trial would likely be gravely at risk.

However, critics such as Ralph Neas, president of People for the American Way, a liberal civil rights advocacy group, are concerned that a military trial might not be as thorough or as fair as an open public trial would be, and that a military jury could convict with a two-thirds vote, rather than the unanimous vote needed in a public trial.

Civil rights leader Jesse Jackson blamed Ashcroft for these decisions, remarking that Ashcroft has "goaded the White House into enacting by executive fiat" a great "encroachment of core American constitutional rights."

President Bush further decided to strip all noncitizens of the right to a public trial, regardless of what crime they might be accused, a move that brought further objection from Jackson: "By executive order, the president has stripped some twenty million people in America of their right to a public and fair trial before a jury of their peers with an attorney of their choice. Anyone who is not a citizen—particularly the millions of hardworking legal residents who have come to this country to pursue their dreams and to seek citizenship—has by executive order been stripped of constitutional rights they once enjoyed."

But times of war and national emergency place the severest of strains on a government, and some of our greatest presidents have made choices under such pressure that they would not make in ordinary times. The delicate balance between civil liberties and national security becomes even more tentative in times of national emergency. The ugly faces of war and terrorism incite many emotions— fear, patriotism, and anger, to name a few—and often cause a strain between a government and its citizens. Mistrust sets in—an often-justifiable mistrust. Loyal citizens who speak their minds can appear to be spies, seditionists, and underground allies of the enemy. Dangerous spies for an enemy nation or terrorist group can appear to be innocent flower shop attendants or teachers or students.

Abraham Lincoln Suspends Habeas Corpus

President Abraham Lincoln (1809–1865) was responsible for one of the most blatant instances of the change in balance during wartime. Faced with the disintegration of the Union, President Lincoln moved to detain a group of suspected enemy sympathizers without due process of law. In fact, he suspended the use of the writ of habeas corpus, which is a key aspect of common law and one of the key supporting pillars upon which the federal government and American civil liberties are built.

"Habeas corpus" is a Latin phrase meaning, literally, "you should have the body," and it describes a type of writ (or order) issued by a judge, requiring, in this case, that a prisoner must be brought before a court or judge to investigate the legality of detaining or imprisoning the accused.

Lincoln was faced with "a clear, flagrant, and gigantic case of rebellion"—the beginning stages of the Civil War. So the president who would later issue the Emancipation Proclamation to set slaves free failed to follow one of the most fundamental of constitutional rights. Under Lincoln's orders (or the orders of U.S. military authorities), hundreds of people were detained without recourse in Northern prisons on suspicion of rebellion. Lincoln considered that he was upholding the Constitution and, in March 1863, Congress came out in support of Lincoln by allowing him to suspend habeas corpus throughout the nation. The cabinet backed him up in September. Even Chief Justice Roger B. Taney of the Supreme Court sidestepped the issue. Generally antagonistic toward Lincoln, in 1857 Taney had led the Supreme Court in the *Dred Scott* decision, holding that no African American had citizenship rights, so Dred Scott, though living in a territory that forbade slavery, could not bring a suit in federal court and was sent back into bondage. Yet now Taney refused to allow treason trials in his court without his presence, which was never possible throughout the ensuing year due to illness. Habeas corpus was effectively blocked by his action. Meanwhile, the Supreme Court decided that an insurrection could be considered equivalent to a declared war, setting the scene for Lincoln, as commander-in-chief, to take actions, such as a blockade, that otherwise would have been unconstitutional without the consent of Congress.

Abraham Lincoln invoked extraordinary powers at a time when the nation was being torn asunder. Some people have thought he was justified. In fact, some point out that the very need to invoke extraordinary powers in time of real emergency can be seen as a sign of the strength of a country's civil liberties. The government of a country with weak civil liberties has no need to seek "extraordinary powers" because such powers are always at hand. Others think that Lincoln overreacted and violated civil liberties by taking this action. In fact, Chief Justice Taney offered this caustic criticism of Lincoln: "I had supposed it to be one of those points in constitutional law upon which there was no difference of opinion that the privilege of the writ [of habeas corpus] could not be suspended except by act of Congress."

Detention without proof of just cause in times of emergency has taken place during several other periods in U.S.

history, notably when martial law was declared in Hawaii following the attack on Pearl Harbor, when Japanese Americans were held in internment camps from 1942 to 1944, and, according to some critics, following the terrorist attacks on September 11, 2001. This injustice has occurred even though the Supreme Court has described the American Constitution as "irrepealable law" intended to hold for both government and citizens and equally in war or peace, protecting "all classes of men, at all times under all circumstances."

Martial Law in Hawaii

On December 7, 1941, Japanese bombers attacked the U.S. naval base at Pearl Harbor in Hawaii, which at that time was a U.S. territory. Like the attacks nearly sixty years later on the Pentagon in Washington, D.C., and the twin towers of the World Trade Center in New York, this unprecedented assault shocked and galvanized Americans.

On the mainland, West Coast cities feared attack at every moment. The reaction in Hawaii was immediate shutdown. The army sought strong controls and the governor immediately complied. He proclaimed martial law, closing bars and restaurants. He suspended the writ of habeas corpus. He closed the civil courts and gave the power to try all criminal cases to the armed forces. But before doing so, he made sure the shift to military rule was temporary, requiring assurances that it would also be short-lived, no more than a few weeks in duration. Things calmed down fairly quickly, and restrictions were lifted one by one as the threat of attack began to wane. A decisive victory in the Midway Islands in the Pacific in June 1942 established U.S. sea power over the Japanese, and nearly all likelihood of attack was put to rest. The bars and entertainment locales by then had been reopened since

February 1942. Yet the military was not ready to reinstall the writ of habeas corpus or to reopen the civil courts.

The struggle between the civilian government of Hawaii and the military generals in charge under martial law went on for years, and was not resolved until after the war ended. A federal judge issued a contempt citation against a general, and the general returned the favor by threatening to court-martial the judge. Finally, the president restored the writ of habeas corpus, and the U.S. Supreme Court stepped in. By the time the struggle concluded, many people had lost weeks, months, and years in unlawful imprisonment.

Internment of Japanese Americans (1942-1944)

Martial law in Hawaii was not the only breach of civil liberties resulting from the attack on Pearl Harbor. Between

AMIDST A JUMBLE OF LUGGAGE IN 1942, THIS JAPANESE-AMERICAN GIRL WAITS TO BE TAKEN TO THE INTERNMENT CAMPS WHERE SHE WILL BE IMPRISONED UNTIL THE END OF WORLD WAR II.

1942 and 1944, the U.S. army summarily detained more than 110,000 Japanese Americans living on the Pacific Coast and moved them to isolated compounds. The move was made in response to pressures from civilian authorities, in particular because of insistence by Earl Warren, who was then attorney general of California. These prisoners, many of whom were American citizens, were singled out because they shared genetic and ethnic heritage with the Japanese enemy forces. Stunned by the attack on U.S. territory in Hawaii, the West Coast states were fearful of espionage and sabotage by residents they thought might be disloyal.

Today, few people deny the gross injustice of this treatment. It is considered a dark time in U.S. history—a blatant example of unjust and harmful racial profiling. Yet racial and ethnic profiling continue to play an important role in law enforcement and, as we shall see, it was one of the three main planks of the U.S. Congress's first, powerful response to the events of September 11, 2001.

Government Reactions to 9/11

As terrorist attacks on the United States on September 11, 2001, stunned the entire country, the federal government quickly took action to protect against follow-up attacks of every kind. The government also sought to find out rapidly who was responsible and bring to justice the perpetrators not already killed in the three suicide airline flights that crashed into their targets: the twin towers of the World Trade Center in New York and the Pentagon in Washington, D.C. A fourth jet plowed into an empty cornfield in Pennsylvania. Thousands of innocent victims were killed, including all the passengers of the four planes piloted by Middle Eastern hijackers.

The government immediately took steps to prevent similar follow-up attacks by grounding all flights in Amer-

PRESIDENT GEORGE W. BUSH AT A WHITE HOUSE SIGNING CEREMONY FOR THE USA PATRIOT ACT, OCTOBER 26, 2001. THE ANTI-TERRORIST BILL AUGMENTED POLICE POWERS FOR SEARCHING AND INVESTIGATING RECORDS, E-MAILS, AND TELEPHONE CONVERSATIONS IN AN EFFORT TO PREVENT FUTURE TERRORISM ATTACKS.

ican airspace, and most Americans were heartened to see safeguards quickly set in place. A Justice Department official rapidly produced a draft of legislation to mend what many felt was a gaping hole in national defenses, and Congress was equally quick to pass it, virtually without having time to read it first. By October 26, 2001, the USA Patriot Act was presented to President George W. Bush for his ready signature.

The details of the Patriot Act brought cautionary comments from civil libertarians. But members of both the administrative and legislative branches stood firm. In testimony before the Senate Judiciary Committee soon after the attacks of 9/11, Attorney General John Ashcroft remarked that those who questioned the government's policies "aid the terrorists." (When he resigned in November 2004, Ashcroft extended his criticism to the federal courts, which he said had endangered national security by ruling against the Bush administration on issues related to the war on terrorism. "The danger I see here," he added, "is that intrusive judicial oversight and second-guessing of presidential determinations in these critical areas can put at risk the very security of our nation in a time of war." These remarks were seen as "dangerous" by organizations such as the ACLU and as valid by most of those present at his speech, a group of conservative attorneys attending the Federalist Society national convention.)

In the weeks following the 9/11 attacks, the Justice Department swept through the country, rounding up people who had immigrated illegally to the United States. A report from the Justice Department's inspector general brought criticisms of the lack of effort to respect civil rights. The report noted the "unduly harsh" conditions, in the words of Inspector General Glenn A. Fine, also citing "significant problems in the way the detainees were handled." A total of more than 1,200 immigrants were arrested—most from Muslim countries—and about half of them were detained on an indefinite basis. Some were reportedly abused both mentally and physically. Prison authorities were slow to allow those detained to consult with their lawyers. When they were allowed to consult their attorneys, the conversations were often bugged by federal investigators, depriving them of attorney-client confidentiality. The number of detainees grew over time to about 1,400. Most were never charged with any crime, and many were released three years later.

The USA Patriot Act did show concern for possible

civil rights infractions and charged the Office of the Inspector General in the Department of Justice with reporting problems. The following two paragraphs are excerpts of a report made September 13, 2004, describing conditions in the Metropolitan Detention Center (MDC) in Brooklyn, New York:

> **While we did not find evidence that detainees were brutally beaten, we did find that some officers slammed and bounced detainees against the wall, twisted their arms and hands in painful ways, stepped on their leg restraint chains, and punished detainees by keeping them restrained for long periods of time. We determined that the way these MDC staff members handled the detainees was, in many respects, unprofessional, inappropriate, and in violation of BOP [Federal Bureau of Prisons] policy.**

> **In addition, we found systemic problems in the way detainees were treated at the MDC, including staff members' use of a t-shirt taped to the wall in the facility's receiving area designed to send an inappropriate message to detainees, audio taping of detainees' meetings with their attorneys, unnecessary and inappropriate use of strip searches, and banging on detainees' cell doors excessively while they were sleeping.**

Perhaps more disturbing to critics, though, was the decision to hold individuals prisoner without explanation. James Zogby, president of the Arab American Institute, an advocacy group for Americans of Arab descent, has asserted,

"The federal government needs to explain what it's doing here, needs to publicly show that these people are planning criminal activity or have engaged in criminal activity, instead of just throwing them in jail and not saying anything."

However, the federal government stood firm. Barbara Comstock, director of public affairs for the Justice Department, stated in June 2003, "We make no apologies for finding every legal way possible to protect the American public from further terrorist attacks." In defense of detentions under the Patriot Act, she added that several federal courts had declared these actions by the government to be completely legal.

Tough Times, Tough Policies

Members of the Senate Judiciary Committee, both Republican and Democrat, met in December 2001 to examine the tough policies presented by the Bush administration and couched in the details of the Patriot Act.

"The Constitution does not need protection when its guarantees are popular," Patrick Leahy, Democratic senator from Vermont and chairman of the Senate Judiciary Committee, reminded his colleagues. "But it very much needs our protection when events tempt us to, 'just this once,' abridge its guarantees of our freedom."

Before the Senate in December 2001, Ashcroft testified that government concern for detainees' rights was considerable. "Our efforts have been crafted carefully to avoid infringing on constitutional rights, while saving American lives," he assured his listeners. Further, he accused them of working for the enemy by voicing concerns for the detainees' civil rights. "To those who scare peace-loving people with phantoms of lost liberty, my message is this: Your tactics only aid terrorists—for they erode our national unity."

The Patriot Act, 2001

The legislation known as the Patriot Act was speedily written and swiftly approved by Congress and the president. The times were urgent, and top speed was required. Its most controversial provisions include:

Section 206: Roving Wiretaps
Section 206 authorizes law enforcement to set up a wiretap on any phone or computer a suspect or target may use. Foreign intelligence authorities can require anyone, such as a librarian, to help with wiretapping, so all users on a library computer could be unknowingly under surveillance because the computer was wiretapped to trap information about one target.

Section 213: "Sneak and Peek"
Known as "sneak and peak," Section 213 enables authorities to conduct investigations without telling the subject either in advance or immediately after the fact—a controversial feature of the Patriot Act. In contrast to many of the act's provisions, this section does not "sunset" (become defunct) in 2005. Authorities are required to advise individuals eventually that they have been the focus of an investigation under this clause, but the delay can be indefinite. The advantage for law enforcement is that the traditional "knock and announce" protocol is no longer necessary and so, unwarned, criminals do not have time to cover up their wrongdoings.

Section 214: Use of "Pen Register/Trap and Trace" Broadened
This modified wiretap technology enables the investigator to trace calls made from a suspect's phone (using pen registers) and monitor the origin of all incoming calls (trap-and-trace technology)—but does not collect the content of the conversation. The Patriot Act requires no warrant for this type of tap if it is alleged to be relevant to an ongoing investigation of international terrorism.

Section 215: Secret Personal Records Searches

Section 215 sets new rules for records searches, allowing authorities to search, without an individual's knowledge or consent, any third-party financial, library, travel, video rental, phone, medical, church, synagogue, and mosque records. This regulation is not popular with librarians, who tend to be protective of an individual's right to read without fear of reprisal.

Section 216: E-mail and Internet-Address Surveillance

This section applies pen register/trap-and-trace authority to Internet surveillance, so dialing, routing, and signaling can be monitored. Its application is also broadened to any information related to an ongoing criminal investigation. In contrast to many of the provisions of the Patriot Act, this section does not "sunset" in 2005.

Section 218: Extending FISA

Section 218 amends the Foreign Intelligence Surveillance Act (FISA), which was enacted in 1978 to enable law enforcement to search in a small number of cases without either a search warrant or probable cause to believe a crime had been committed. The Patriot Act expands the number of cases to which this exception applies to any instance in which the government can allege there is a foreign intelligence basis for the search. Also, the search may be conducted secretly and may be authorized by a secret court that has no accountability to the Justice Department and is unknown to the public. FISA was originally conceived to give the administration leverage against foreign spies. Now it can also be used against Americans.

Sections 411 and 412: "Alien and Sedition Acts"

According to Section 411, anyone associating with a terrorist, even unknowingly, may be deported. Section 412 states that the attorney general need not show that an alien is dangerous or obtain a court ruling to that effect before briefly detaining him or her. The Patriot Act does not authorize the most problematic actions taken by the Bush administration against aliens, including indefinite detentions, use of military courts, detention in secret military brigs, detention without explanation, and general secrecy.

Section 505: National Security Letters

This section allows the attorney general (or a delegated individual) to subpoena personal records by sending a "national security" letter. This is a subpoena directly from the administration. No judge or court order is required, and the recipient need not be suspected of any crime (no probable cause required). Before the Patriot Act such letters were reserved for those suspected of being spies. Now they can be sent to anyone, including American citizens. In contrast to many of the provisions of the Patriot Act, this section does not "sunset" (become defunct) in 2005.

Section 802: "Domestic Terrorism"

Section 802 establishes a new category of crime: domestic terrorism, which is described as activities that endanger human life and are in violation of U.S. law, as well as those intended to influence government policy through intimidation or coercion.

In July 2003, legislation known as the "Otter Amendment" to the Patriot Act was passed in the U.S. House of Representatives by a vote of 309 to 118. It was introduced by C. L. "Butch" Otter of Idaho, a conservative Republican, and its purpose was to retract funding from the Patriot Act's "sneak and peek" provisions. Other members of Congress have proposed changes in the Patriot Act, and some commentators claim that opposition to the Patriot Act exists across the political spectrum.

President George W. Bush and Attorney General Alberto Gonzales stand firmly by the Patriot Act and have vowed, as of March 2005, to seek an extension beyond its 2005 sunset. This legislation, says Bush, has leveled the playing field between terrorists and law enforcement agents. As a result, he says, law enforcement agents have broken up many al Qaeda cells and arrested would-be terrorists.

An Associated Press article carried by the *Sacramento Bee* on November 16, 2003, reported that Ashcroft "tried to assure lawyers . . . that the Bush administration welcomes oversight and is using new powers to make 'quiet, steady progress' in the terrorism fight."

The government's post-9/11 treatment of individuals suspected of terrorist acts had inspired criticism even among the gathering of conservative lawyers known as the Federalist Society—especially the imprisonment of "enemy combatants" against the United States, secrecy concerning the identity and charges against the many immigrants arrested, and the Guantánamo, Cuba, detention of individuals suspected of terrorist acts.

The government, Ashcroft said, was acting in these instances for the purpose of "protecting the American people while honoring the Constitution and preserving the liberties we hold dear."

Conservative Anti-"Patriot"

Some conservatives asserted that if they thought the Patriot Act and other surveillance precautions were "essential responses to the terrorist attacks of September 11, 2001," and were "specifically tailored to meet such threats in the future . . . , perhaps then one could accept some of the encroachments on civil liberties as necessary and perhaps even worthwhile," wrote columnist and former U.S. Representative Bob Barr in the online publication of *The American Spectator*. However, he bluntly added, "But they are not."

Barr pointed out that the agencies that could have prevented the 9/11 attacks never took responsibility, never apologized. Instead they blamed Congress for lack of support and asked for more power and more money. Bullied in this way, Congress handed over "nearly whatever they asked for." Barr would have supported increases of power and funding that were "narrowly tailored, limited, or designed only to correct those specific provisions of existing laws that needed to be tweaked."

Instead he saw a wide-ranging increase in broad powers—many restrictions against wiretapping lifted, fewer controlled search-and-seizure procedures approved. He believes the executive branch used the September 11 attacks as leverage to push into law a set of measures its members had long sought to pass—without success.

The result is heightened power in Washington to gather evidence within national borders, for the purpose of recognizing terrorists in our midst. However, in Barr's view, these tactics are unlikely to derail attacks by terrorists.

Summarizing, Barr concludes,

> **The real way to catch terrorists is with better intelligence gathering, better coordination and analysis, better utilization of existing law enforcement tools, and quicker and more appropriate dissemination of that intelligence. The key word is better. With a few notable exceptions, the USA Patriot Act is a legislative grab bag that does little to encourage better law enforcement and intelligence work. Instead, we have an unprecedented expansion of federal law enforcement powers that significantly diminishes the civil liberties of American citizens, with only marginal increases in real security.**

He describes this loss of civil liberties as a "dramatic alteration to the very foundation of our society."

Restriction of Rights and Undue Power

Other critics also see grave threats to civil liberties inherent in the USA Patriot Act and other measures taken by the federal government in the thirty-six months following 9/11. Jonathan Turley, a professor at George Washington University Law School, has posed the question, "What would happen if you woke up living in a quasi-police state?" Turley does not think the question is a pointless query, given the direction government has moved in the aftermath of 9/11. "Major changes," he writes, "have come in small, incremental steps, with each privacy right or civil liability concern balanced in isolation against the potential of a massive attack."

He describes post-9/11 U.S. public policy as a study in pointillism, the branch of impressionist art associated with the French painter Georges-Pierre Seurat. Seurat created images out of thousands of tiny, individual dots of color, which he massed in such a way that a scene emerged, a sort of precursor of computer imagery created from pixels of color. Each dot alone is a small, distinct blob of color. But when the viewer steps back, the eyes seem to "connect the dots" to form a picture.

Turley recounts the following list of "dots" in which he sees an ever more urgent warning that government actions on behalf of security are endangering the bulwark of civil liberties:

- Imprisonment of citizens for an indefinite period and without recourse to counsel or courts.

- Collecting intelligence about library and Internet records.

- Wiretapping privileged conversations between attorneys and clients.

- Development of a plan to establish a "national reporting system" whereby citizens would report on each other's day-to-day actions.

• Creation of an enormous computer database to track all purchases made, from medical expenses to groceries to computer equipment.

• Heightening surveillance and increasing searches without adherence to Constitutional restrictions.

• Assuming the right to use a military tribunal system to execute accused individuals without recourse to the provisions of the Constitution or to federal laws.

• Development of a plan for a national identity card.

• Suggesting that the states pass laws that would allow governors to declare martial law in the event of an emergency without approval from any other branch of the government.

• Use of military forces for domestic police work.

• Endorsing the broad use of assassination as an alternative to capture, including the possible assassination of citizens.

• Ignoring the Geneva Convention in selected instances.

Restricting Civil Liberties to Ensure American Safety

Pluses:

• Curtailment of civil liberties is necessary in view of the extreme need for security.

• The majority of Americans say they are willing to give up some or all of their civil liberties in exchange for security.

• Flexibility enables a government to make short-term adjustments to cover emergencies.

• There is historical precedent for temporarily curtailing some civil liberties in a time of emergency; while regrettable, it has seemed necessary from time to time.

Minuses:

• Temporarily curtailed liberties may be permanently lost.

• The action of curtailing liberties creates the sense that they are optional and can be interrupted at any time.

• For individuals wrongly imprisoned or otherwise deprived of liberty, the lost months and years are never regained.

Protecting Privacy versus Watching for Trouble

Of the three key activities used by the federal government today to stop would-be terrorists in their tracks, two—intelligence gathering and intelligence sharing—can be seen as invasions of the privacy of the innocent. They can also be seen as necessary elements of the fight against terrorism, and they are important to the strategies so far developed by the U.S. Department of Homeland Security.

Based on investigations carried out after the terrorist attacks on September 11, 2001, experts quickly concluded that the federal government had not coordinated and used its intelligence effectively. No federal agency had called attention to the fact that members of a terrorist group known as al Qaeda had entered the country and plotted the September 11 massacres. Not the FBI, and not the CIA. Congress and other officials came to what seemed an obvious conclusion: information gathering and analysis needed improvement, and they needed it fast. Most of the American public agreed to the premise, with some voices counseling caution.

According to author and editor James D. Torr, "In general Americans want the government to use its power to investigate and avert terrorist threats, but at the same time they oppose the idea of a 'police state' in which the government continuously monitors average people."

Right to Privacy: Sharing Intelligence

The second mainstay of post-9/11 homeland security is networking among the intelligence agencies, the sharing of information to bring the big picture into focus. The knowledge that one member of a known terrorist group was training to pilot a jet airliner was one sign. The knowledge that several had pursued this unusual undertaking should have rung a cacophony of bells. Yet no one agency had collected these pieces of information. And the separate agencies—the FBI, the CIA, and the National Security Agency (NSA)—did not communicate with each other, so no one had "connected the dots."

To remedy this gaping glitch in communication, Congress passed the Homeland Security Act, signed into law November 25, 2002. In the most thoroughgoing reorganization of the federal government since the creation of the Department of Defense by President Harry Truman's administration in 1947, this law created the Department of Homeland Security (DHS). The department's leader, called a secretary, was also designated as a member of the cabinet and the department was charged with coordinating the information collected by the more than twenty agencies that comprise it, as well as the FBI and the CIA.

The agencies included under the authority of DHS include many areas of authority, from the U.S. Coast Guard (charged with protection of coastal waterways and ports), the Federal Emergency Management Agency (FEMA, in charge of response to disasters), the Secret Service (assures the safety of the president and other officials, as well as investigating financial crimes such as counterfeiting), the Border Patrol, and the Bureau of Citizenship and Immigration Services (replacing the former Immigration and Naturalization Service, or INS).

Major areas of concern for the Department of Homeland Security are reflected in its major sections, called directorates, which cover border, immigration, and transportation issues; emergency preparedness and recovery, including chemical, biological, radiological, and nuclear attacks; and research, information analysis, and protection of the infrastructure, such as bridges, nuclear power plants, and communications systems.

The two related agencies that still remain outside the authority of DHS are the FBI and the CIA, although these two formerly completely independent organizations are now expected to cooperate and share information with DHS agencies.

Of the two, the FBI has older roots, dating back to the formation in 1908 of a select cadre of investigators within the Department of Justice. Today, the FBI, a division of the Department of Justice, is the federal government's chief investigative agency. The FBI has collected and maintained a centralized crime information database, including fingerprints, which it shares with other law enforcement agencies. It also supplies laboratory technology and services for analysis of criminal evidence. Above all, the FBI is responsible for investigating crimes involving federal laws and protection from foreign intelligence collection and terrorist acts.

The CIA, on the other hand, is a much more recent addition to the U.S. government's federal armor. CIA responsibilities focus on national security in particular. This agency, formed in 1947, gathers information and carries on secret operations intended to protect against foreign knowledge of critical national secrets. It also coordinates the operations of other intelligence agencies, including the Defense Intelligence Agency (DIA) and the National Security Agency (NSA).

Cyberspace Surveillance

The Patriot Act as passed in 2001 afforded federal investigators unprecedented access to online communications taking place between American citizens. However, federal officials assert the surveillance has been respectful of privacy while functioning effectively in the cause of security. The legislation allows investigative access to e-mail messages and the power to monitor Web sites visited by suspects. Investigators are not allowed to observe the content of these communications, however.

Before the Patriot Act was passed, some surveillance of telephone calls was allowed—police could trace the source of incoming calls and the recipient of outgoing calls, but not listen to the content. So the Patriot Act simply extended an already existing method of surveillance to online communications. Investigators were permitted to know e-mail addresses and URLs that suspects used in the same way they already could avail themselves of phone numbers used. A further restriction stipulated that, while these methods can be used without a warrant, this can be done only with reference to an ongoing investigation.

In 2002, *Wall Street Journal* reporter Daniel Pearl was kidnapped and murdered in Pakistan while covering news during the height of the U.S. military action in Afghanistan. Federal Deputy Assistant Attorney General Alice Fisher pointed out that in 2003 U.S. prosecutors succeeded in finding out who was responsible for Pearl's death by using the surveillance methods made possible by the Patriot Act.

Assuring skeptics of the government's concern about privacy, Fisher added, "We have been using this tool, and we have been very cautious not to get into content." She said that the government has used the surveillance provisions of the Patriot Act "effectively, aggressively, and responsibly," adding that she was unaware of any instance in which a violation of privacy had occurred.

However, critics remained unsure because of the secrecy under which the government was functioning. Lee Tien, senior counsel for the Electronic Frontier Foundation, pointed out the unlikelihood that the Justice Department would discuss attempts they had made that were not successful. Tien lacked any evidence that privacy had been violated, and yet he also lacked evidence that it had not. However, Tien noted that combined broad surveillance powers coupled with secrecy "raises privacy and accountability problems because the amount of information that can be gathered is significant."

Another cyberspace-oriented directive of the Patriot

Act charges the government with establishing biometric criteria for face recognition. Software developed by the Commerce Department would be used at border checks and in other settings where identification of suspects is important—including racial profiling.

Ethnic and Racial Profiling

The study of modus operandi (mode of operation) and other crime patterns in a case has long been a mainstay of police investigations. As police investigators watch a criminal's pattern play out—and as they gather more information of other kinds—they are often able to identify an individual perpetrator by watching for behavior that matches pieces of the crime pattern.

Similarly, groups of people, or types, may have habit patterns, characteristics, or favorite fashions in common. Intellectuals often wear glasses; men with long, unkempt hair who drive beat-up cars may be more dangerous in a dark alley; a muscular Asian man may be accomplished at martial arts. But these are only assumptions, and sometimes these assumptions may be unfair.

Such is the case when police stop a driver just because he is black or Hispanic or of Middle Eastern appearance. Ethnic and racial profiling came into close scrutiny in the 1990s, with several cases of videotaped beatings of minorities by law enforcement officers.

In the months and years following the events of 9/11, ethnic and racial profiling have become more common. Civil libertarians, however, oppose this broad-stroked approach to national security problems.

Critics also expressed concern that the government kept some detainees imprisoned for weeks, even months, without establishing any connection between them and terrorist groups. For example, detainees included a physician from San Antonio and an Arab-American citizen from Evansville, Indiana, who happened to have a pilot's license. (The latter was under suspicion because the government thought Middle Eastern men were trying to rent crop duster airplanes.)

Ashcroft went on record saying that the "aggressive detention of lawbreakers and material witnesses" has evidently been effective in deterring fresh attacks. And Kent Scheidegger, legal director for the Criminal Justice Legal Foundation (a conservative organization advocating reduced rights for accused and convicted criminals), points out that, without more information, investigators need to look at and talk to a lot of people to get a sense of who the perpetrators are and where and by whom the next attack will take place.

Extreme Danger Requires Extraordinary Measures

Many politicians and citizens alike argue that times of extreme danger to national security require a special dispensation, a suspension of some civil liberties in favor of measures of surveillance, imprisonment without explanation or due process of law, ethnic profiling, and other restrictions and infringements.

Some point out that, although some such moves in the past have later been declared unfair and unconstitutional (as in the case of the Japanese-American internment), liberties lost have later been regained.

Civil libertarians argue, however, that reparations are little solace to those who have lost chunks—weeks, months, often years—of their lives. Gestures of regret and atonement don't bring back that lost time, nor do they begin to repay financial losses or compensate for the emotional pain experienced by such victims.

IN THE EARLY 1930s THE WOMEN'S ORGANIZATION FOR NATIONAL
PROHIBITION REFORM AND OTHERS USED POSTER CAMPAIGNS TO
ADVOCATE REPEAL OF THE EIGHTEENTH AMENDMENT (1919),
WHICH PROHIBITED THE MANUFACTURE, SALE, OR TRANSPORTATION
OF INTOXICATING LIQUORS. THE CAMPAIGN AND ITS POSTERS
PERSUASIVELY ARGUED THAT PROHIBITION HAD MISFIRED,
ENCOURAGING CRIME AND CORRUPTION INSTEAD OF TEMPERANCE.

Senator Dianne Feinstein (D-California), who chairs a Senate subcommittee assessing the Patriot Act's impact, takes this pragmatic viewpoint: "If the new tools in this act are working and effective, clearly we should keep them and perhaps strengthen them. If they are being abused, we should eliminate them or add new safeguards."

Pluses:

• The Justice Department considered the Patriot Act "a crucial weapon in the war on terrorism," according to spokesman Charles Miller.

• Continuing threats and attacks show, former Attorney General John Ashcroft pointed out, that "the worldwide terrorist threat is real" and therefore that the expanded power of law enforcement agents is warranted.

• Officials of the Justice Department contend that critics misinterpret the extent of investigative powers given to the Federal Bureau of Investigation to examine library records; according to the Justice Department, these powers are in effect solely if a case is part of an investigation into international terrorism, and then only with the consent of a federal judge.

• The Patriot Act, according to Ashcroft, establishes "a new ethos of justice, one rooted in cooperation, nurtured by coordination and focused on a single, overarching goal: the prevention of terrorist attacks."

• The Terrorist Screening Center (TSC) was launched to consolidate terrorist watch lists and provide continual operational support for federal, state, and local screeners and law enforcement. The FBI has established a new executive director for intelligence and specially trained intelligence analysts. The Department of Homeland Security Information Network is connected to all fifty states and more than fifty major urban areas, and allows information sharing among thousands of local agencies and the Homeland Security Operations Center.

• The dramatic increase in information sharing allowed by the Patriot Act has enabled law enforcement to find and dismantle terror cells in Portland, Oregon; Lackawanna, New York; northern Virginia; and other locations.

• Warrants are now applicable across state and district lines, eliminating the need to obtain multiple warrants for the same person—a lengthy process that previously hindered counterterrorism efforts.

• Law enforcement officials now have better tools to fight terrorism, including roving wiretaps and the capacity to seize assets and end financial counterfeiting, smuggling and money-laundering.

• In sum, the president's White House Homeland Security Web page says, "This

legislation has prevented terro
and saved American lives."

Minuses:

• Decisions made in an emergency are often concluded hastily and without proper consideration. After September 11, 2001, members of Congress pressed for a rapid response with strong legislation, but then later regretted some aspects of the resulting USA Patriot Act.

• As one of Benjamin Franklin's favorite mottoes states: "They that can give up essential liberty to obtain a little temporary safety deserve neither liberty nor safety."

• Critics on both the left and the right object that the Patriot Act gives law enforcement agencies more power than they need.

• Critics also caution that the Patriot Act oversteps Constitutional provisions for privacy rights and such personal liberties as due process of law, freedom from unreasonable searches and seizure, and exemption from imprisonment without clear cause.

• Widespread, deep concern about loss of civil liberties due to the U.S. Patriot Act and other post-9/11 measures resulted in the passage of resolutions objecting to the legislation and refusal to uphold it by more than 379 communities in forty-three states, including six statewide resolutions, in Alaska, Hawaii, Idaho, Maine, Montana, and Ver-

se communities
2 million people
Patriot Act.

onstitutional the
y involved in the
3I to examine in-
and make other
rds of American
ney Ann Beeson,
ould not have to
worry that the FBI is rifling through their
medical records, seizing their personal papers, or forcing charities and advocacy
groups to divulge membership lists."

• The U.S. government is based on an effective set of checks and balances coupled with
a strong commitment to basic individual
civil rights that together ensure a balance of
power. Following the 9/11 attacks, the government has not focused sufficiently on preserving citizens' individual rights and the
system of checks and balances that prevents
any one area of government from gaining
too much power.

The controversy that accompanies all the issues discussed in this chapter gives rise to intense emotion. In such
a moment in history the challenges to our country's
courage and strength are enormous. As Nadine Strossen,
president of the American Civil Liberties Union, and her
colleagues wrote passionately in their testimony on "Security and Liberty" before the National Commission on Terrorist Attacks Upon the United States:

America faces a crucial test. That test is whether we—the political descendents of Jefferson and Madison, and citizens of the world's oldest democracy—have the confidence, ingenuity and commitment to secure our safety without sacrificing our liberty.

For here we are at the beginning of the twenty-first century, in a battle with global terror. Terrorism is a new and different enemy. As a nation, we learned this on September 11, 2001, when a group of terrorists attacked us here at home, and within the space of minutes murdered nearly 3,000 of our fellow Americans and citizens of other nations, innocent civilians going about their everyday lives.

What Are Civil Liberties?

During the latter decades of the eighteenth century, a tattered group of colonies along the Atlantic seaboard of the North American continent began what Benjamin Franklin called "the American experiment" in self-government. Moored in the works of English philosopher John Locke and Anglo-American political philosopher Thomas Paine, the United States of America was born at the height of the "Age of Reason," also known as the "Enlightenment," a time noted for its growing respect for reason, science, and humanity. A precursor of the Age of Reason, *Two Treatises on Government* (1690) was written by John Locke, who put forth the idea that the people, not the state, held sovereignty—a radical idea in a time when many governments were absolute monarchies. Locke promoted "natural law," as he called it, and he spoke out for the rule of the majority and government as protector of its citizens and their *natural rights*. This was a fairly new idea, one that Thomas Paine would develop further a century later. Paine's two-volume work, *Rights of Man* (1791–1792), also declared that all humans have natural rights, and he listed those that most people now consider the most basic: liberty, property, and security. Preservation of these rights, he said, was the purpose of all political associations.

Both Locke and Paine greatly influenced the framers of the American Declaration of Independence and the founders of the United States government. Out of the carefully reasoned thinking of that time, the American colonies and most of Europe and England came to endorse the concept of "natural rights," a cousin of the "certain inalienable rights" of the American Declaration of Independence, the rights outlined in the American Bill of Rights. These ideas took root in American soil for many reasons. American colonists were tired of getting the short end of every deal, sick of toiling to line the pockets of businesses and monarchies across the seas. They wanted something better: a government that was less subject to abuse, one that operated more fairly for everyone.

Prior governments—the medieval European monarchies of the eleventh to thirteenth centuries—had based their foundations on the concept of a monarch who ruled by divine right. So whatever the whim of the monarch, his or her decisions were God's will. The monarch's power was passed from generation to generation as a birthright. This arrangement worked reasonably well during the reign of a fair and just king or queen. But under a petty, mean-minded, greedy monarch, life throughout the domain could be miserable. What recourse did subjects of the realm have?

However, by June 15, 1215, King John of England had already put his seal to a document known as the "Magna Carta," or "Great Charter." In this document the king promised to abide by the traditions of feudal law in dealing with his subjects. It was not a democratic or egalitarian document, but it defined the relationship between the monarch and the nobility, a treaty that was binding on both sides. The agreement set a precedent in English law, establishing that even the king was subject to legal restraints; his subjects had rights described by law and he put in writing his promise to abide by the law. This aspect of English law affected the laws of all countries influenced by England, including the thirteen colonies along the Atlantic coast of North America.

The governments of other nations were slower to feel this influence, but by the 1700s many philosophers and thinkers in such countries as France, Switzerland, Germany, and the British Isles—including Voltaire, Rousseau, Paine, Jefferson, and others—began to recognize that by using their rational powers they might fashion systems of government based on the claimed existence of certain fundamental human rights—rights that came as a birthright to every living human being.

The idea of human rights was in the air in eighteenth-century continental Europe, Great Britain, and the American colonies. It grew naturally out of the intense philosophical examination of human existence and the roles of government. Tyranny tended to benefit the few who were in power. A more rational approach, according to Enlightenment thinkers, would benefit many more. Out of this premise came the idea of "civil rights" and "civil liberties"—rights and liberties granted to individuals by government. Or, more accurately, rights and liberties laid aside by society for individuals as sacrosanct territory upon which government must not transgress.

In the nineteenth century, British philosopher John Stuart Mill (1806–1873) had a very important influence on the development of civil liberties. He talked about what he called "one very simple principle" controlling the appropriate assignment of powers to the state and to individuals. "That principle is," he explained, "that the sole end for which mankind are warranted, individually or collectively, in interfering with the liberty of action of any of their number, is self-protection. That the only purpose for which power can be rightfully exercised over any member of a civilized community, against his will, is to prevent harm to others. . . . Over himself, over his own body and mind, the individual is sovereign."

What Are the Basic Rights?

The American Declaration of Independence lays out the existence of three inalienable rights: life, liberty, and the pursuit of happiness. This was a good start, yet the terms are vague. Later, the first ten amendments to the United States Constitution refined the concepts into a "Bill of Rights." These set forth the basic rights we think of today:

- Freedom of religion (freedom of belief or nonbelief)

- Freedom of speech and freedom of the press

- The right to form and attend public gatherings

- The right to bear arms

- Freedom from searches of property without a specific search warrant

- Freedom from imprisonment without due cause

Later, after the War Between the States (the Civil War), three more rights were added by Amendments Thirteen, Fourteen, and Fifteen, with a fourth, Amendment Nineteen, added in 1920:

- Freedom from slavery or involuntary servitude

- The obligation of the state governments to honor the freedoms set forth in the federal Bill of Rights

- The right to vote, regardless of race, creed, or color

- The right to vote regardless of gender

Where Do Civil Liberties Come From?

By what authority do we conclude that these are "inalienable rights," that these are areas of power where the individual must receive deference from the government? Three major lines of thought have grown up to explain the source of these civil liberties. Before the 1700s most European thinkers were affiliated with religious institutions, and they almost universally asserted that all citizens received these rights directly from God. This view seemed correct to many thinkers at the time, from philosophers to clergy and from peasants in the farm fields to generals on the battlefields. By looking to God, they reasoned, they marshaled a power they considered greater than any human individual or group.

But with the Age of Reason in the eighteenth century, a more secular view of government developed, a view that did not revolve around religion. If government was to serve all its

KING JOHN SIGNING THE MAGNA CARTA IN 1215.

citizens, and if freedom of religion (including the right not to embrace religious causes) was to be one of the founding principles, the concept of certain "inalienable rights" had to function effectively for everyone. So, many philosophers turned to "natural" rights. This line of thought allowed the concept of civil liberties to include both religious and nonreligious citizens. However, even this more inclusive concept seemed too vague and restrictive to some experts on constitutional law.

Alan M. Dershowitz, a professor at Harvard Law School and one of the foremost American scholars on civil liberties, makes a case for a different point of view in his book *Shouting Fire: Civil Liberties in a Turbulent Age* (2002). Dershowitz sees civil liberties as a product of history, derived from positive law and experience. That is, rights become established by law and through the record of judicial judgments. Dershowitz points out that an ethnically diverse democracy cannot serve all its citizens equally based on "God-given" rights, since wide-ranging differences in beliefs exist among the populace.

"The first claimed external source of natural rights is God," writes Dershowitz. "But experience has demonstrated that the natural rights of the Bible and other holy books can be cited by the devil as well as by conservatives and liberals." God's law has been called upon to justify slavery, the genocide of American Indians, anti-Semitism, terrorism, and many other atrocities.

Many Enlightenment thinkers favored the idea of "natural" human rights based on universally shared values. However, this concept turns out to be vague and elusive. Human values tend to vary from culture to culture and from era to era. They reflect a wide range of contrasting thoughts and mores, and finding the "natural" common denominator is difficult if not impossible. Thinkers from Spinoza to Einstein have questioned the existence of any set of universally shared natural values. As Spinoza wrote, "Nature has no goal in view, and final causes are only human imaginings."

But if rights are not thought of as either God-given or natural, then what is their source? Human judgment and wisdom? To many people this seems like a shaky concept. If we see rights as simply made up or invented by people, what will keep them from being tossed aside by some tyrant or special-interest group that lays claim to a greater wisdom?

These are questions that even the finest legal thinkers find daunting. One expert, Ronald Dworkin, has proposed that rights must be discovered, not invented. He sees the "best political program" as "one that takes the protection of certain individual choices as fundamental, and not properly subordinated to any goal or duty or combination of these." Operating from basic premises like these, he and other supporters of natural law contend that just laws are preexistent in nature. The job of legal thinkers is to uncover the existence of these natural laws or underlying moral principles.

Dworkin's view opposes most aspects of the legal positivist approach, which sees a legal system simply as a construction, the sum of its own rules, and holds that no connection necessarily exists between a body of laws and moral principle.

The Birth of Civil Liberties in the United States

When the framers of the U.S. Constitution wrote their final draft in 1787, they did not include a list of guaranteed individual rights. Their intent was to set up a limited federal government. However, when the new Constitution began its rounds for ratification by each state, unease grew over the lack of a statement of fundamental rights. The Constitution won ratification in its original form, but pressure for compromise caused the First U.S. Congress to consider the addition of a bill of rights. As a member of the House of Representatives, James Madison spearheaded the idea and drew extensively from the English Bill of Rights and the Virginia Declaration of Rights written by Virginia-born statesman George Mason. After revision by

The Bill of Rights
(Actual Text)

First Amendment

Congress shall make no law respecting an establishment of religion, or prohibiting the free exercise thereof; or abridging the freedom of speech, or of the press, or the right of the people peaceably to assemble, and to petition the Government for a redress of grievances.

Second Amendment

A well regulated Militia, being necessary to the security of a free State, the right of the people to keep and bear Arms, shall not be infringed.

Third Amendment

No Soldier shall, in time of peace be quartered in any house, without the consent of the Owner, nor in time of war, but in a manner to be prescribed by law.

Fourth Amendment

The right of the people to be secure in their persons, houses, papers, and effects, against unreasonable searches and seizures, shall not be violated, and no Warrants shall issue, but upon probable cause, supported by Oath or affirmation, and particularly describing the place to be searched, and the persons or things to be seized.

Fifth Amendment

No person shall be held to answer for a capital, or otherwise infamous crime, unless on a presentment or indictment of a Grand Jury, except in cases arising in the land or naval forces, or in the Militia, when in actual service in time of War or public danger; nor shall any person be subject for the same offence to be twice put in jeopardy of life or limb; nor shall be compelled in any criminal case to be a witness against himself, nor be deprived of life, liberty, or property, without due process of law; nor shall private property be taken for public use, without just compensation.

Sixth Amendment

In all criminal prosecutions, the accused shall enjoy the right to a speedy and public trial, by an impartial jury of the State and district wherein the crime shall have been committed, which district shall have been previously ascertained by law, and to be informed of the nature and cause of the accusation; to be confronted with the witnesses against him; to have compulsory process for obtaining witnesses in his favor, and to have the Assistance of Counsel for his defence.

Seventh Amendment

In Suits at common law, where the value in controversy shall exceed twenty dollars, the right of trial by jury shall be preserved, and no fact tried by a jury, shall be otherwise re-examined in any Court of the United States, than according to the rules of the common law.

Eighth Amendment

Excessive bail shall not be required, nor excessive fines imposed, nor cruel and unusual punishments inflicted.

Ninth Amendment

The enumeration in the Constitution, of certain rights, shall not be construed to deny or disparage others retained by the people.

Tenth Amendment

The powers not delegated to the United States by the Constitution, nor prohibited by it to the States, are reserved to the States respectively, or to the people.

The Bill of Rights
(Interpreted)

The Bill of Rights includes the following basic civil liberties:

First Amendment
Prohibits the U.S. government from establishing an official religion and guarantees freedom of religion, speech, press, and assembly. This amendment also establishes a right to request the government to respond to complaints.

Second Amendment
Affords the right to bear arms.

Third Amendment
Prevents the government from quartering horses and soldiers in people's homes. (This restriction resulted from invasive practices employed by the British during the colonial period. It was an important issue at the time, but has not been a problem since the end of the Revolutionary War in 1783.)

Fourth Amendment
Prevents unlawful search and seizure, prohibiting police or other government agents from searching or seizing individuals' property without evidence that a crime has been committed and without a search warrant specifically describing the area to be searched and the items or persons to be seized.

Fifth Amendment
Protects against arbitrary government actions in five ways: A grand jury must formally bring charges prior to prosecution of an individual for a federal crime. (Exceptions exist for those in military service during wartime or times of public danger.) One may be tried only once for any crime. No one may be compelled to testify against himself. No one can be deprived of life, liberty,

or property by the government without due process of law. And just payment is to be made when private property is taken for use by the public.

Sixth Amendment
Provides for rights for the accused in a criminal prosecution, including the right to a speedy public criminal trial by an impartial jury, the right to know why and of what one has been accused, and to meet and hear those testifying for the opposition, as well as the right to counsel and to witnesses for the defense.

Seventh Amendment
Provides the right to trial by jury in civil suits and invokes the procedures of common law regarding retrial.

Eighth Amendment
Prevents the imposition of excessively high bail and fines.

Ninth Amendment
Stipulates that citizens may retain other rights not enumerated in the Bill of Rights.

Tenth Amendment
Reserves either to the states or to the people any power the Constitution does not attribute to the federal government and does not deny to the state governments.

a committee of the House of Representatives, the final document was debated and passed by the House, then pared down by the Senate to twelve amendments, further refined by a joint committee, and passed by Congress in 1789. During the ratification process, Vermont became the fourteenth state, raising to eleven the number of ratifications required to add the Bill of Rights to the Constitution. That number was reached in 1791, when it passed, appropriately enough, in the state of Virginia.

These amendments were originally applied only to federal issues, but later, a series of Supreme Court decisions in the 1980s established that the Bill of Rights extend to the states as well.

How Do Civil Rights Differ from Civil Liberties?

People often use the terms "civil rights" and "civil liberties" interchangeably, but since the time of the Civil Rights movement in the United States in the 1960s, the term civil rights has become identified with the African-American fight for equal consideration before the law and, by extension, recognition of equal rights for other groups, including women, Asian Americans, Latinos, Jews, Jehovah's Witnesses, gays and lesbians, people with disabilities, and so on. This set of rights revolves around obtaining equal protection against discrimination—in housing, employment, public accommodations, and administration of criminal justice.

Most rights specialists consider civil rights, interpreted in this way, as a subset of the more general set of rights known as civil liberties, which includes First Amendment rights, due process of law, and privacy, as well as the group of amendments known as the Post-Civil War Amendments, Amendments Thirteen, Fourteen, Fifteen, and Nineteen (although the last was added later, as mentioned, in 1920).

David and Goliath

Alan Dershowitz argues that, "based on our experience over time, we should prefer to live in a society in which the government is denied certain powers, such as the power to censor speech, even deeply offensive speech." He believes that history (the story of human experience) illustrates that a democratic society that recognizes basic rights—which he lists as "uncensored expression, freedom of conscience, due process, democracy, and equal protection of the laws"—provides a better living environment than one that does not.

Basically, the concept of civil liberties establishes areas where the power of the government is restricted out of deference to individuals. Some interpreters of the Bill of Rights contend, further, that these rights of the minority over the majority should prevail even if they do not benefit the general community over the long haul. These literalists demand a strict interpretation of Constitutional law: If one begins to bend the law, what is to stop a tyrant from wantonly tossing aside civil liberties and individual freedoms?

Meanwhile, other critics feel that interpretation of Constitutional law should be sensitive to the mores of the time. The Supreme Court and other courts have frequently made decisions that many people found objectionable, or even odious—for example, decisions that allow for the public burning of an American flag to convey an opinion, for animal sacrifice as part of a religious observance, or for the right of a group of Nazis to conduct a public demonstration. All these decisions raised controversy because they seemed inherently out of step with socially acceptable behavior.

Members of the Supreme Court, however, take the view that their job is to rule in favor of the letter and spirit of the law to the best of their knowledge and wisdom. An

The Post-Civil War Amendments

(Actual Text)

Thirteenth Amendment

Neither slavery nor involuntary servitude, except as a punishment for crime whereof the party shall have been duly convicted, shall exist within the United States, or any place subject to their jurisdiction. . . .

Fourteenth Amendment

All persons born or naturalized in the United States, and subject to the jurisdiction thereof, are citizens of the United States and of the State wherein they reside. No State shall make or enforce any law which shall abridge the privileges or immunities of citizens of the United States; nor shall any State deprive any person of life, liberty, or property, without due process of law; nor deny to any person within its jurisdiction the equal protection of the laws . . .

Fifteenth Amendment

The right of citizens of the United States to vote shall not be denied or abridged by the United States or by any State on account of race, color, or previous condition of servitude. . . .

Nineteenth Amendment

The right of citizens of the United States to vote shall not be denied or abridged by the United States or by any State on account of sex. . . .

individual justice may find an interpretation as objection-able to his or her set of personal preferences as some critics do. But that visceral reaction cannot be the basis for a Supreme Court decision. Instead, the justices are bound by a keen sense of the overall picture and the breadth of hu-man liberty called for by the Constitution. They are not competing in a popularity contest. That is why their ap-pointments are for life—so they have no need to be popu-lar. They don't have to win an election by pleasing their constituency. They do not need to gain an appointment. Instead, ideally at least, they can set out to try each case as fairly as possible, using rational thinking and logic as their best tools.

At the same time, bias is a human trait, and Supreme Court justices are human. Typically, justices carry some ideologies into the Court, and if no counterbalances from their colleagues offset those biases, the country could be forced to—because of lifetime appointments—live with a long period of biased judgments.

The Supreme Court

The courts act as interpreters of the Constitution and the Bill of Rights. Because the words used in these documents are somewhat general, vague, and open to interpretation, the Supreme Court has the responsibility for deciding questions such as "What is speech?" or "What is due process of law?" or "What is cruel and unusual punish-ment?" based on the mores and circumstances of the time. At one time, for example, the death sentence was a matter of course, although some methods of execution were thought "cruel and unusual." Today, fewer and fewer na-tions use capital punishment, although several states in the United States still allow for a death sentence. In early 2005, the U.S. Supreme Court handed down a decision against capital punishment for juveniles. However, the Court was not declaring capital punishment unconstitutional in any broader sense. A few weeks later, the Court declined to grant a stay of execution to an adult Ohio inmate. Each of these decisions required careful consideration and close interpretation of the law as it applied to each case.

The Constitution does not specifically grant the Supreme Court the power to interpret the Constitution, but this role has grown more important and central through the years. Usually, the Supreme Court rules in cases appealed from the lower courts. Over time, through their decisions, the Supreme Court justices have produced a body of case law (the development of law by interpretation, forming a body of legal precedents from which future cases may be decided by analogy). These decisions serve to define and interpret the provisions of the Bill of Rights and the Constitution.

This process began in 1803 with the case of *Marbury* v. *Madison*, the first to require an interpretive role. Just before the end of his term in 1801, President John Adams made a series of fifty-eight last-minute appointments to give his political party greater strength. Among those were several judiciary appointments for which the commissions were not delivered before the next president, Thomas Jefferson, took office. Jefferson didn't want members of the opposing party holding these appointments, and he told his Secretary of State, James Madison, to hold back some of the commissions. As a result, one of the appointed men, William Marbury, sued Madison, requesting the Supreme Court to order Madison to give him his commission. Supreme Court Chief Justice John Marshall saw the opportunity to shape the role of the Court as interpreter of law. The court refused by a vote of five to zero to order delivery of the commission—not because Marbury did not deserve it but because the law that allowed them to give such an order was unconstitutional, according to the Court's own decision. Thus the Court gave up a small amount of power to gain a much larger portion of power: the Supreme Court would serve as the final court of review and interpretation of law.

The decision raised a multitude of questions about the Supreme Court and its role, how extensive its power should be, the importance of checks and balances in constitutional government, and how it should all work together.

For the most part, the Supreme Court has cast its interpretation in broad terms. For example, the First Amendment begins: "Congress shall make no law respecting . . ." But the Supreme Court has interpreted the First Amendment restrictions to apply as fully to the executive branch and the states as they do to the U.S. Congress.

Some conservatives think that this reading of the First Amendment does not reflect the original intent, while other analysts have pointed out that the flexibility of interpretation has been one of the great assets of the American form of government.

Civil Libertarianism as a Nonpartisan Value

In political discussions, people often mistakenly assume the "turf" of civil liberties to be either a conservative concern or a liberal concern, the property of the political right or left. However, civil liberties are everyone's concern, and members of the left are as likely as those on the right to consider them either unimportant (when they don't favor the speaker's opinions) or important (when they do), regardless of political leanings.

In her book *Free for All: Defending Liberty in America Today*, writer and civil libertarian Wendy Kaminer writes, "Civil libertarianism is a nonpartisan virtue, just as repressionism is a nonpartisan vice." That is, society in general benefits from mutual recognition of the value of civil liberties equally for everyone, regardless of political persuasion. "What distinguishes libertarians," Kaminer continues, "is a focus on preserving fair processes rather than obtaining particular results."

During the 1920s, the government supported conservative views about alcohol consumption with the Prohibition Act and established censorship for films. And again, in the 1950s, a campaign led by Senator Joseph R. McCarthy against communist subversion also targeted hundreds of individuals thought to have leftist leanings (many of whom were not guilty of any form of subversion). However, in the 1990s, Kaminer points out, several left-leaning college administrators "promulgated repressive speech and sexual misconduct codes and, with little due process, prosecuted students for political incorrectness." And then conservatives objected in the name of civil liberties.

Should Civil Liberties Sometimes Be Sacrificed?

One individual's positive civil liberty often may conflict with someone else's negative civil liberty. On a simplistic level, one neighbor's right to enjoy peace and quiet (a negative: absence of noise) in his home may conflict with another neighbor's right to run her noisy lawn mower (a positive: the right to make noise). The merits of each side of a case must be weighed in enacting a law or deciding a court case, and many factors may come to play in the overall decision.

Racial equality rings true today, but in the 1950s, not everyone saw the rightness of it. The segregationist position was a keystone for an entire segment of Southern society, and it proved very difficult to abandon. The very

McCarthyism

In the early 1950s, Congress became intensely concerned with the prospect that subversive agents had infiltrated throughout the United States, and they sought them out in every walk of life, from schoolteachers to doctors, lawyers, and newspaper editors, from radio to the movies, and from military generals to private industry. By 1953, three congressional committees were involved: the Senate Permanent Investigations subcommittee (chairman: Senator Joseph R. McCarthy), the subcommittee of the Senate Internal Security Committee (chairman: Senator William E. Jenner), and the House Un-American Activities Committee (HUAC) (chairman: Representative Harold H. Velde).

The findings of all three committees gained the spotlight, but Senator McCarthy's fervency brought him worldwide attention. His assertion in 1950 that communists had permeated the State Department brought his name to the attention of the general public. In fact, his fame grew so great that a new "ism" was born: McCarthyism. He also became the center of a controversy over his tactics. The 1953 *Collier's Yearbook* summed it up: "To his supporters, McCarthyism is the essence of American democracy, its fundamental defense; to his enemies, it is the beginning of dictatorship, the destroyer of all civil rights and the best friend Communism has in the world today."

McCarthy thought he saw subversion in the Voice of America (a U.S. government-funded radio news service broadcasted in dozens of languages worldwide), the Government Printing Office, and the armed forces, and his investigations and the work of the other committees spread to schools, colleges, and churches as well.

The ensuing effort to identify possible subversives resulted from the high-pressure realities of international Cold War politics. The Cold War was a post–World War II struggle between the communist regime of the Union of Soviet Socialist Republics (USSR or the Soviet Union) and the United States and its allies. The strain between the two factions was enormous, often falling just short of engaged military conflicts. Communism is a natural opponent of capitalism, and animosity between the USSR and the Western allies dated back to the birth of the Soviet Union in 1917. Now, in the 1950s, the specter of potential nuclear holocaust intensified the tension.

Yet, many of America's European allies and people in the United States criticized the tactics used by the three congressional investigative committees, and McCarthy's leadership in particular came under fire. What was the purpose of the committees? To some critics, their work seemed primarily to fulfill political goals of the committee members. Furthermore, the committees had no system in place that protected the civil liberties of those who testified. The committees even published information about those accused, often without evidence, in many cases ruining their careers. Many actors and directors in the movie industry were unable to obtain jobs for years following publicity about political beliefs that they may not have actually held. In many cases the accused neither intended nor did any harm. Finally, while communism was at odds with capitalism philosophically, McCarthy and the investigative committees greatly magnified the threat and struck unwarranted fear in the hearts of many Americans.

McCarthy never uncovered evidence that substantiated his 1950 charge of communist infiltration in the State Department. In April 1954, his accusations centered the spotlight on the secretary of the army, who, he said, had concealed foreign espionage activities. The army in turn made accusations about McCarthy. Senate investigations ensued, which were closely covered by radio and television. Although McCarthy was cleared of all charges in the end, the Senate censured him for the methods he had used in his investigations.

Ironically, in the 1990s, after the end of the Cold War and the collapse of the Soviet Union, archives of information began to open up, allowing historians to examine communications between the Soviet government and its spies in the United States. They discovered that, during World War II alone, some 350 Americans did indeed act as spies for the Soviet Union—some of them in high places. So McCarthy was right to suspect a problem, but virtually everyone agrees he conducted his investigation both inhumanely and ineffectively.

existence of slavery and bias manifested by segregation in the colonies and the country that formed from them is a shameful chapter in our history, but like it or not, some people's liberties were sacrificed in the process of undoing the injustice. Today many people ask, how could a national government based on such a strong, progressive Bill of Rights have taken so long to secure all these rights for the entire population?

The same question applies to women and the right to vote, with the Nineteenth Amendment not ratified until 1920—just the most obvious of the many inequalities between the genders that existed nearly without comment for most of two centuries.

Should Civil Liberties Be Expanded?

A concept known as "victims' rights" sprang up in the 1990s, building on the idea and the vocabulary of basic inalienable rights and civil liberties—and expanding the idea of positive and negative rights. Initially, the concept grew out of a sense that in criminal prosecution all the protections listed in the Bill of Rights and the post–Civil War amendments were piled on the side of the criminal suspect. The accused is protected against unreasonable searches by the government, double indemnity, self-incrimination, and so on. Meanwhile, what about the victim? No consideration or recourse is offered by these documents for the victim, who may have suffered immeasurably. This valid concern nonetheless confuses the concept of civil liberties. In fact, the Bill of Rights and the post–Civil War amendments are intended to protect individuals not against each other but against representatives of the government who might otherwise act unjustly.

Moreover, the trend ballooned and "victims' rights"

became applied to many other realms, such as subjection to secondhand smoke, loud snoring, perfume worn in public, and a host of other wrongdoings. Sociological issues, moral questions, interpersonal problems—all became expressed in terms of "rights."

An expanded list of these rights might include the right to be protected from pornography, the right of a gay couple to adopt children, the right not to be exposed to secondhand smoke, and the right to anonymity. However, none of these rights relate to allocation of power to individuals versus members of government—which is the domain of civil liberties.

Real rights are more enduring than these somewhat faddish concerns. Unlike a limited railroad ticket, as Justice Robert Jackson once said, rights are not just good for one train at one particular time and day only. Rights belong to all people for an extended period of time.

Government as Big Brother

It is easy to become caught up in the idea that our lives would be ideal if only everyone thought the way "we" do. This is true of both conservatives and liberals. Conservatives tend to think the government should discourage or prevent various activities considered immoral, corrupt, or otherwise objectionable by a large segment of the population. Liberals tend to think the government should discourage prejudice in speech and action. We fear what others will do if they are allowed freedoms, and want to restrict what they say or do to what is acceptable to us. Most people believe they themselves should be free to do what pleases them—but they fear the consequences if their neighbors have the same rights. They are fearful of freedom. "Left and right," says Wendy Kaminer, "people expect government to keep them safe and to make their neighbors more virtuous."

We turn naturally to state power to help when our lives are not safe. If you cannot safely go out in your neighborhood, if you cannot travel in your country without fear, if your children are not safe at school, you are not free. So, safety has a key role in the land of the free. And government, with its military power and its many other resources, has a key role in our safety. But there are paths that government does not have a mandate to travel, and making your neighbors more virtuous (however you define virtue) may be one of them.

A poll taken by the *Washington Post* in November 2001, after the terrorist attacks of September 11, showed that a majority of those surveyed approved of the controversial order given by the president that established a plan to use secret trials conducted by military tribunals for any noncitizen suspected of supporting or engaging in terrorism. Almost 90 percent supported secret detention of the some six hundred immigrants already imprisoned by November (the number later grew to more than double that).

On April 19, 1995, a massive bomb exploded in a truck parked in front of a federal building in Oklahoma City. The blast, a deadly terrorist act, killed 168 people and destroyed most of the building, including many surrounding structures. After the bombing, a poll showed that 65 percent of people questioned in 1995 favored giving a go-ahead to the FBI for infiltrating and observing groups suspected of terrorist intentions, even though no crime had been committed. The idea of deporting noncitizens suspected of planning terrorism was favored by 58 percent of those asked (even though Timothy McVeigh, the perpetrator of the Oklahoma City bombing, was a U.S. citizen). And 54 percent said that in the fight against terrorism, the government should not be concerned about impairing individual rights. In the struggle to find a balance between safety and liberty, people tend to think in terms of safety first. The question is, perhaps, how can we protect both our security and our freedom?

Freedom of Speech

The right to speak one's mind freely became the heart of the First Amendment to the Constitution, the first of the group of ten amendments that became known as the Bill of Rights. Expanded to include freedom of the press and symbolic speech, the freedom to express oneself is arguably the most powerful and important—the keystone of all civil liberties. It is the main thoroughfare for sorting out differences and achieving effective compromises. It provides an environment that nourishes communication through free and open debate about contrasting points of view. Without the First Amendment provision of freedom of speech, books like this one might not exist.

Initially, only the U.S. Congress was required to honor the right to free speech. However, in a Supreme Court decision handed down in *Gitlow* v. *New York* in 1925, the states were declared to be subject as well, thanks to the stipulations of the Fourteenth Amendment, which states in part that "no state shall make or enforce any law which shall abridge the privileges or immunities of citizens of the United States."

Before discussing that case, the Supreme Court had ruled only on cases involving the federal government. *Gitlow v. New York*, however, turned on a state law that declared it a crime to advocate the overthrow of the government. Gitlow was declared guilty—but in the process of delivering their decision, the justices also ruled that, based on the Fourteenth Amendment, the protections of the First Amendment applied at the state level as well as the federal level.

This or similar interpretations of the Fourteenth Amendment have been invoked many times since then, but not everyone agrees on this interpretation. Some constitutional experts—especially states' rights proponents—either oppose the Fourteenth Amendment in part or entirely, or favor "selective incorporation," applying only "fundamental rights" against the states.

Historically Speaking

Freedom of speech has not always received a strong embrace. It had to be won. Historically, in England as elsewhere in Europe, the Crown—whether worn by king or queen—was always right. Or rather, it was supposed to be that way. Criticism of the king or any of his court was considered sedition, the crime of disloyalty, of dissent. It was a crime punishable by prison or death. In 1476, the arrival of the printing press in England brought technology into the picture, bringing changes with it that rivaled for that day what computers have done in our time. Now publishing and distributing ideas in books, reviews, journals, letters, essays, and so on became much easier. Written speech could reach many corners of the kingdom and control was much more difficult. Yet, for the rest of the 1400s, the 1500s, and much of the 1600s, English royalty made every attempt to remain in control by licensing both the presses and all publications. Without a license, nothing could be published.

In 1642, civil war broke out, and King Charles I was deposed by Parliament and its leader, Oliver Cromwell, a Puritan with very strict religious views. So, while royalty no longer imposed its shortsighted views, during the reign of Parliament an even tighter rein restrained the flow of ideas through a series of restrictive laws.

In response and in defense of a free press and freedom of speech, the great English poet John Milton wrote *Areopagitica: A Speech for the Liberty of Unlicensed Printing to the Parliament of England*. (The title refers to Areopagus, the hill in Athens where the tribunal met.) In it, Milton ardently pleads the case for freedom of the press. He counts the losses involved in suppressing even the most licentious and tainted books. Learning is lost, he says, and people lose the ability to discuss and debate intelligently. Furthermore, objectionable ideas are never really suppressed successfully in this way. People talk and pass heretical thoughts on to the common people. "Evil manners," he points out, "are as perfectly learnt without books a thousand other ways which cannot be stopped. . . ." One might just as effectively try to impound a flock of crows by shutting the park gate, he adds. Finally, Milton concludes that censorship is not only ineffective—it is also very costly, limiting as it does the variety of concepts that can enter into the "marketplace" of ideas and contribute to the richness of thought.

Colonial Journalists Seeking Freedom

However, especially when it came to questions of political opinion, politicians in office were inclined to object to dissenting views of their conduct. And they had the power to make life most uncomfortable for a dissenter in both seventeenth- and eighteenth-century England and the colonies. Benjamin Harris was a journalist and bookseller who encountered this sort of trouble in London, England, in the seventeenth century, where his highly political pamphlets were held to be seditious (inclined to incite an insurrection or resistance of authority). So in 1686 he fled to escape steep fines and imprisonment and emigrated to the colonies, like many others, looking for the freedom to be himself. He settled in Boston, where he established a bookstore combined with a coffee shop, which attracted local philosophers and book lovers.

On September 25, 1690, he published his first (and last) American newspaper, which, ironically, the colonial governor immediately suppressed for containing content that he considered both offensive and dangerous. That was both the end of Harris's colonial newspaper career and the last Boston would see of a regularly published local newspaper for fourteen years. Harris, however, continued to publish, and before 1690 he produced the only elementary primer textbook to exist in America for the next fifty years.

Benjamin Franklin's brother James, also a newspaper publisher, found himself running afoul of the government in 1721 when he questioned the safety of a smallpox vaccine in his Boston newspaper, the *New-England Courant*. In the process he was critical of the governor and other leading citizens of the community. And he was just warming up. The authorities issued an order to cease publication, but Franklin refused and wound up in jail. But the *New-England Courant* kept on coming—now with brother Ben standing in as publisher.

Franklin won the day, however. By now discontinued, licensing was no longer an issue. When Franklin's case came before a grand jury, no action was taken against him for continuing to publish his paper even though it had been banned. Thus, Franklin's case set one of the earliest precedents for the premise that government cannot prohibit publication *before* it takes place.

This premise was tested more recently, in 1971, when

Benjamin Harris, First British-American Journalist

Writing and publishing was a tough business in the late seventeenth century, and Benjamin Harris played rough. An Anabaptist (member of an unorthodox Protestant sect) and Whig (a political radical), he wrote scathing attacks on Roman Catholics and Quakers in England in the early years of his career. In 1679, he joined Titus Oates in what Oates called the Popish Plot, a tale fabricated by Oates claiming that Roman Catholics were plotting the murder of Charles II in order to place the king's Roman Catholic brother James on the throne. The hoax was later discovered, but not before some thirty-five innocent people were executed.

By 1686 Harris decided his best course was to flee to the British-American colonies. On September 25, 1690, he published the first American newspaper, *Publick Occurrences, Both Foreign and Domestick.* Its news consisted of a range of snippets: a report of an outbreak of smallpox, news of a suicide, rumors about the king of France, and thoughts on the tide of relations with neighboring American Indians. The last was where he got in real trouble.

The governor was displeased by Harris's description of the Indians—trusted allies of the governor—as "miserable savages, in whom we have too much confided." He had also failed to obtain the proper licensing, which had been required in Massachusetts since 1662. So, the paper he had planned to bring out monthly or even more often in the event of "any Glut of Occurrences," never saw another issue.

A journalist at heart, however, Harris returned to London in 1695, where he published the *London Post* steadily from 1699 to 1706.

researcher Daniel Ellsberg leaked a controversial document called *The Pentagon Papers* to the *New York Times* and the *Washington Post*. President Richard M. Nixon went to the courts to stop the newspapers from publishing it, since it was a sensitive, top-secret study of misrepresentations made to the public regarding U.S. involvement in the Vietnam War. However, in *New York Times v. United States* the Supreme Court ruled that constitutionally neither the president nor the courts had the power to prevent publication.

English legal expert Sir William Blackstone summed up the position in the mid–1700s: "The liberty of the press is indeed essential to the nature of a free state; but this consists in laying no previous restraints upon publications, and not in freedom from censure for criminal matter when published."

Seditious Libel—or Free Speech?

The case of newspaper publisher John Peter Zenger is considered a major early landmark on the road to freedom of the press in the United States. While Harris lost his battle in the late seventeenth century and James Franklin won his contest, the story of John Peter Zenger was the first victory from which freedom of the press would ultimately take root. As University of Missouri at Kansas City law professor Douglas Linder describes it, "The Zenger trial is a remarkable story of a divided Colony, the beginnings of a free press, and the stubborn independence of American jurors."

Born in Germany in 1697, John Peter Zenger left Germany in 1710 with his family when he was thirteen and settled in the colony of New York after a two-month voyage across the Atlantic to America. His father died during the trip, so he and his siblings were raised by their mother. Without the choice of following in his father's occupation, Zenger became apprenticed to New York's only printer, William Bradford, from whom he learned the trade. He

COPIES OF JOHN PETER ZENGER'S *WEEKLY JOURNAL* WERE PUBLICLY BURNED IN NOVEMBER 1734 BY ORDER OF THE COLONIAL GOVERNOR OF NEW YORK.

completed his apprenticeship in 1718 and married a year later. However, Zenger's first wife died shortly after giving birth to a son, and in 1722, Zenger married Anna Maulist, who would later figure in his fight for freedom of the press.

Zenger and Bradford formed a partnership in 1725; however, a year later Zenger had gone into business for himself. As one of the only two printers in town, he eked out a living printing primarily religious tracts, pamphlets, and brochures. The only newspaper in New York, the *New York Gazette*, was published by Bradford.

William Cosby arrived in New York from England on August 7, 1731, as the newly appointed colonial governor. The portrait of him that emerges from historical accounts shows him to be both opportunistic and tyrannical. From the time he arrived, he tried to latch onto funds for himself that rightfully belonged to Rip Van Dam, a New York statesman who had filled in for him in an interim capacity. Cosby also attempted to fix an election and hired a propagandist to take over final approval on all editorial content of the sole newspaper, the *New York Gazette*.

Cosby's quarrel with the seventy-one-year-old Van Dam did not go well. Cosby attempted to have the case tried without a jury by directing the three-member provincial Supreme Court to try the case. The matter escalated into a legal dispute over substituting a trial by this court for the well-established system of trial by jury. The justices were not unanimous in Cosby's favor. Asked by the governor for an explanation, dissenting Chief Justice Lewis Morris unexpectedly gave, not a private accounting, but a pamphlet made available to the public. It was printed, of course, by the only printer in the colony who was not in Governor Cosby's pocket: John Peter Zenger.

Irate, Cosby fired Morris, heating up the opposition even more. Van Dam and Morris joined forces with James

Alexander, a dynamic and persuasive attorney from Scotland. The three formed a new political party, to be known as the Popular Party, to represent the rising tide of opposition to the status quo.

Alexander, sometimes known as the "mastermind" of the Popular Party, founded a newspaper to bring focus on political issues from the party viewpoint. He called it the *New York Weekly Journal* and he asked Zenger to print it (since his was the only other newspaper competing with the Cosby-controlled *Gazette*). Alexander also wrote most of the opinion pieces, news, and commentary that Zenger published in the newspaper.

When the governor tried to pack the Assembly with assemblymen favorable to his regime, the Popular Party was ready. On election day, November 4, 1733, Cosby was particularly focused on the race for assemblyman from Westchester—where his nemesis, Lewis Morris, was contesting the governor's favorite. Assuming that Quaker voters would cast ballots for Morris, Cosby had the sheriff disqualify Quakers from voting in the election by stipulating that all voters had to swear the oath required of everyone at the time—they could not just "affirm," as Quakers had commonly been allowed to do before, in keeping with their religious beliefs. Ironically, Morris won without the disallowed Quaker votes.

The first issue of the *New York Weekly Journal* came out the next day, November 5, 1733. It plainly told the story of Cosby's attempt to rig the election, including this account of the sheriff's part in it:

> [T]he sheriff was deaf to all that could be alleged on that [the Quaker] side; and notwithstanding that he was told by both the late [former] Chief Justice and James Alexander, one of His Majesty's Council and counselor-at-law, and by one William Smith, counselor-at-

law, that such a procedure [disqualifying
Quaker voters for affirming, not swearing]
was contrary to law and a violent attempt
upon the liberties of the people, he still
persisted in refusing the said Quakers to
vote. . . .

In commentary thought to be written by James
Alexander, the *Weekly Journal* continued its attacks on
Cosby and spoke out for liberty of the press and its corner-
stone position among all liberties:

The loss of liberty in general would soon follow the suppression of the liberty of the
press; for it is an essential branch of liberty,
so perhaps it is the best preservative of the
whole. Even a restraint of the press would
have a fatal influence. No nation ancient or
modern has ever lost the liberty of freely
speaking, writing or publishing their senti-
ments, but forthwith lost their liberty in general and became slaves.

Within two months Cosby began his efforts to remove
this source of constant attack. He tried to bring pressure
upon the Grand Jury in January 1734 to indict the *Journal*
for breaking the law of seditious libel (publication of defamatory remarks that might incite an insurrection or resistance
of authority). The Grand Jury refused. He tried again in November. The Grand Jury again declined, pointing out that
the authorship of the articles was not clearly known.

Cosby announced a reward of fifty pounds for discov-
ering who the author was. He also ordered a public burning of Zenger's newspapers to discredit them. Then he tried
to get around the refusals returned by the Grand Jury and
obtained a bench warrant from his two accomplice justices.
The sheriff arrested Zenger on November 17, 1734, and

imprisoned him in the Old City Jail in New York, where Zenger remained incarcerated for eight months.

The *Journal*, due out the next day, missed an issue, but only one. The next issue, published by Zenger's wife, Anna, contained an apology and explanation from Zenger for the missed issue. Though pressured for information about who wrote the *Journal*'s content, Zenger refused to reveal the authorship. His work ethic and integrity earned him respect and the exorbitant bail set at eight hundred pounds earned him sympathy. If Cosby had thought he would put the *New York Weekly Journal* out of print so easily, he must have been sorely surprised.

Furthermore, Zenger's lawyer, sixty-year-old Andrew Hamilton, was considered the best in the colonies. (Two previous attorneys were disbarred under pressure from Cosby.) After further efforts from Cosby to rig the outcome, the jury was selected, and the trial began on August 4, 1735. Following a surprise statement by Hamilton that his client did not deny printing and publishing the remarks at issue, a silence fell upon the court.

Finally, the attorney general spoke, calling for a quick verdict of guilty, since Zenger confessed, in essence, to publishing the remarks. He added that the truth of the remarks was an inadequate defense in the case of libel, which was the case at the time under English law.

At which point, Zenger's attorney, Andrew Hamilton, argued that surely no one could rightly interpret the law as meaning to prohibit "the just complaints of a number of men who suffer under a bad administration." Aware that they were trying a landmark case with much at stake, he explained at some length that the libel law of England should not rule in America. He did not have much to back up his position, although he was eloquent. But, as one might expect, Chief Justice James Delancey ruled against allowing presentation of evidence that the statements published in Zenger's newspaper were true—since Delancey considered that point irrelevant. "The law is clear," he pronounced, "that you cannot justify a libel."

Delancey also suggested that the jury could choose to consider only the evidence concerning whether Zenger published the material and leave the legal question of libel to the justices. To that, Hamilton made his own counter move, pointing out to the members of the jury that they had the power to judge both aspects of the case. Why, his discourse implied, would they give up that power?

Finally, Hamilton pointed out the great importance of the case, which he told the jury was nothing less than the question of a free press and the natural right to criticize abuses by those in power. Hamilton concluded:

> The question before the Court and you, Gentlemen of the jury, is not of small or private concern. It is not the cause of one poor printer, nor of New York alone, which you are now trying. No! It may in its consequence affect every free man that lives under a British government on the main of America. It is the best cause. It is the cause of liberty. And I make no doubt but your upright conduct this day will not only entitle you to the love and esteem of your fellow citizens, but every man who prefers freedom to a life of slavery will bless and honor you as men who have baffled the attempt of tyranny, and by an impartial and uncorrupt verdict have laid a noble foundation for securing to ourselves, our posterity, and our neighbors, that to which nature and the laws of our country have given us a right to liberty of both exposing and opposing arbitrary power (in these parts of the world at least) by speaking and writing truth.

The jury retired to deliberate and returned shortly with a verdict of "Not guilty." The courtroom was jubilant, Hamilton was feted and sent home triumphant to Philadelphia, and Zenger was freed at last.

No laws were changed as a result of the Zenger trial, but the seeds of an important idea were planted: freedom of the press. Fifty years later, as the Bill of Rights was being penned, Lewis Morris's grandson, Gouverneur Morris, was one of the framers of the Constitution. At that time he wrote this comment: "The trial of Zenger in 1735 was the germ of American freedom, the morning star of that liberty which subsequently revolutionized America."

Enter the First Amendment

In rebellion against English attempts to control speech and publications in the colonies, the framers of the Constitution were adamant about securing freedom of speech and freedom of the press near the top of the list of rights. As a result, in contrast to the English and early colonial experience, the U.S. government position today is that, with some exceptions such as fighting words and libel, punishment for the contents of a publication or speech is generally considered unconstitutional. Nor can speech or writings be censored or punished *prior* to publication, as the James Franklin case showed.

Alien and Sedition Acts (1798)

Among the early challenges to First Amendment rights was a series of moves made by Congress to protect the administration of John Adams from criticism during a time when the threat of war with France was intense. Named the Alien and Sedition Acts of 1798, the four laws addressed internal U.S. security issues by placing pressure on immigrants and ignoring provisions of the First Amendment. They were enacted amidst the XYZ affair, when the U.S.

narrowly avoided war with France over an attempt made by French Foreign Minister Talleyrand to obtain bribes in exchange for a peace settlement. (In fact, an intense naval battle, known as the "quasi-war," did occur, but Adams managed to avoid a declared war, which could have been a disaster for the young nation.)

The first of the Alien and Sedition Acts required immigrants to reside in the United States for fourteen years (an increase of nine years) before becoming eligible for citizenship. It was repealed in 1802. A second measure, the Alien Act, provided for deportation of foreign-born residents, expiring in 1800. A third, the Alien Enemies Act, called for arresting and deporting all aliens from a nation with which the United States was at war. Aimed primarily at French immigrants of the time (since the country was trembling on the verge of war with France), as well as Irish immigrants (who had been critical of the Adams administration), this act is now rarely used.

The fourth, the Sedition Act of 1798, was later thought to be unconstitutional, and both James Madison and Thomas Jefferson were secretly behind resolutions in Virginia and Kentucky that reserved the right to declare all four acts null and void in those states as a protest against the limitations on civil liberties set by the four laws together. The Sedition Act called for curtailing the rights of the press, making printing or publishing dissenting opinions a criminal offense. Aiding a foreign power to plot against the United States, opposing the lawful acts of Congress, and publishing any false, malicious, or scandalous statements about the federal government brought punishment of up to five thousand dollars in fines and up to five years' imprisonment.

Today these laws are considered unconstitutional. Why were they enacted? Historians point out that members of John Adams's government were aware that military successes in Europe had been secured by the groundwork of insurgents within the enemy borders. So they enacted these measures to protect national security against such enemy maneuvers within the borders of the United States—an example showing that unconstitutional measures can often seem reasonable in the heat of a crisis.

Speech Expanded

Some people define free speech very literally as the right to talk out loud and audibly, in person, about your thoughts. Over time, however, the right to free speech has become expanded, through court decisions, to include certain actions, sometimes referred to as "symbolic speech." Looking at speech in this sense, what makes an act self-expressive, or symbolic? If an action qualifies as symbolic, what makes it allowable or disallowable?

Some insight into these questions can be gleaned from Supreme Court decisions, such as one case that set a precedent in 1951 for discerning the difference between an arrest for disorderly conduct and protected freedom of speech.

Feiner v. New York

Irving Feiner's arrest took place on March 8, 1949, when he refused to obey a police order to end his discourse on African-American rights before a street-corner crowd of about seventy-five racially mixed listeners. A student in Syracuse, New York, Feiner had been heard by police to say, "The Negroes don't have equal rights; they should rise up in arms and fight for their rights." Attending police also heard him add, "President Truman is a bum," "The American Legion is a Nazi Gestapo," and other mildly insulting remarks.

The crowd muttered and jostled a bit, but did not seem disorderly, although it overflowed the sidewalk. Finally, one of the listeners threatened a police officer, saying that if he didn't get Feiner off the corner, he would. That's when Feiner was asked to move on, refused, and got arrested. He was convicted of inciting a breach of the peace. This was confirmed on review by two New York courts, and the Supreme Court upheld these decisions. However, the dissenting opinion by Justice William Orville Douglas brought to light a different point of view, the opinion that a young student had been thrown in jail for expressing unpopular ideas. In the words of Justice Douglas:

Public assemblies and public speech occupy an important role in American life. One high function of the police is to protect these lawful gatherings so that the speakers may exercise their constitutional rights. When unpopular causes are sponsored from the public platform, there will commonly be mutterings and unrest and heckling from the crowd. When a speaker mounts a platform it is not unusual to find him resorting to exaggeration, to vilification of ideas and men, to the making of false charges. But those extravagances do not justify penalizing the speaker by depriving him of the platform or by punishing him for his conduct.

A speaker may not, of course, incite a riot any more than he may incite a breach of the peace by the use of "fighting words." But this record shows no such extremes. It shows an unsympathetic audience and the threat of one man to haul the speaker from the stage. It is against that kind of threat that speakers need police protection. If they do not receive it and instead the police throw their weight on the side of those who would break up the meetings, the police become the new censors of speech. Police censorship

has all the vices of the censorship from city halls, which we have repeatedly struck down.

Flag Burning

In keeping with the concept that "speech" in the larger picture really encompasses all expression of ideas and feelings, First Amendment protection for free speech evolved into protection for gestures, wearing of symbols, and expressive or symbolic actions.

One of the most visceral and emotional issues is the act of burning or desecrating the United States flag. Many Americans think that the flag, as a symbol of our country, should be protected. In 2001, forty-eight of the fifty states had statutes on the books criminalizing flag desecration. Yet the Supreme Court has twice ruled that any law protecting the flag violated First Amendment protection.

It began with Gregory Lee Johnson, a citizen of Texas, who participated in a political demonstration outside the 1984 Republican National Convention in Dallas. He was protesting against some of President Ronald Reagan's administrative policies as well as the corporate policies of several businesses based in Dallas. After marching with a group of other protestors, Johnson burned an American flag to accompanying chants of watching protestors. Several onlookers were offended by the demonstration, but no one was hurt.

Johnson was arrested, convicted of desecrating a venerable object, and sentenced to one year in prison and a fine of two thousand dollars. His first appeal—to the state court of appeals—was rejected. However, the Texas Court of Criminal Appeals declared this application of the Texas statute unconstitutional. The court found that Johnson had engaged in expressive conduct when he burned the flag, so he was protected by the First Amendment and *in this case*, the state could not "rope off" the flag as a protected symbol of

GREGORY LEE JOHNSON SET A PRECEDENT IN 1984 BY
BURNING AN AMERICAN FLAG TO PROTEST THE REPUBLICAN
NATIONAL CONVENTION TAKING PLACE IN DALLAS. ALTHOUGH
JOHNSON WAS ARRESTED BY THE STATE OF TEXAS AND
CONVICTED OF FLAG BURNING, THE TEXAS COURT OF APPEALS
OVERTURNED THE VERDICT. WHEN THE STATE OF TEXAS TOOK
ITS CASE TO THE U.S. SUPREME COURT, THE COURT UPHELD
THE TEXAS COURT OF APPEALS, DECLARING THAT JOHNSON'S
FLAG BURNING WAS A PROTECTED FORM OF COMMUNICATION,
KNOWN AS "SYMBOLIC SPEECH."

national unity. Consequently, the Supreme Court granted certiorari (a writ from a higher to a lower court to obtain records so a case can be reviewed).

Addressing the question of whether Johnson's conduct was protected, the Supreme Court rejected "the view that an apparently limitless variety of conduct can be labeled 'speech' whenever the person engaging in the conduct intends thereby to express an idea," but acknowledged that conduct may be "sufficiently imbued with elements of communication to fall within the scope of the First and Fourteenth Amendments." In deciding whether particular conduct possesses sufficient communicative elements to bring the First Amendment into play, the Court queried whether Johnson was trying to convey a particular message and whether it was likely to have been understood. According to the Court, "Under the circumstances, Johnson's burning of the flag constituted expressive conduct, permitting him to invoke the First Amendment. The State conceded that the conduct was expressive. Occurring as it did at the end of a demonstration coinciding with the Republican National Convention, the expressive, overtly political nature of the conduct was both intentional and overwhelmingly apparent."

Texas made the point that the flag symbolized the national identity and unity, and that attacks upon it called all that it symbolized into question. But the Court was not moved. "If there is a bedrock principle underlying the First Amendment," according to the Court, "it is that the government may not prohibit the expression of an idea simply because society finds the idea itself offensive or disagreeable."

Later in 1989, Congress passed the Flag Protection Act, which outlawed flag burning. The act was struck down as unconstitutional by the Supreme Court the following year. In recent years several attempts have been made to amend the Constitution to protect the flag, but so far nothing has come of that venture.

Sexual Content, Pornography, and Obscenity

Censorship, like most civil liberties issues, is complex. Most censorship begins with the idea of protecting children from speech or writing or art or photographs or Web pages—any form of expression—that contain disturbing material. Even many adults prefer not to be confronted against their choice with disturbing forms of expression. Many libertarians feel that censorship is a "slippery slope"—once one starts down the slope, one rapidly finds oneself sliding and tumbling all the way to the bottom. However, many people feel the need for some forms of censorship.

Some of the most controversial First Amendment issues surround censorship of sexually oriented material. The federal government has historically taken a conservative, restrictive position on materials with any sexual content, for example with the 1873 Comstock Act, which banned from the U.S. Postal Service all material dealing with the topic of birth control. Up until the 1950s, many U.S. cities censored movies shown within city limits, requiring each film to be approved and licensed by city officials.

Literature with sexual themes has received First Amendment protection since the 1930s, with the trend set in part by James Joyce's highly acclaimed novel *Ulysses*. However, by 1957 the Supreme Court had established that obscene material does not have First Amendment protection. In *Roth* v. *United States* and *Alberts* v. *California* (both in 1957), the Court established this set of guidelines:

1. "All ideas having even the slightest redeeming social importance—unorthodox ideas, controversial ideas, even ideas hateful to the prevailing climate of opinion—have the full protection of the guaranties, unless excludable because they encroach upon the limited area of more important interests; but implicit in the history of the First

Amendment is the rejection of obscenity as utterly without redeeming social importance."

2. Sex and obscenity are not the same. Obscene material deals with sex in a manner "appealing to prurient interest"—that is, "material having a tendency to excite lustful thoughts."

3. In judging obscenity, the court used the following criterion: to the average person, applying contemporary community standards, does the dominant theme of the material, taken as a whole, appeal to prurient interest?

By 1973, the court had worked out a further refinement known as the "Miller test": In addition to evaluation as an "appeal to prurient interest" for an "average person," the material shows or describes sexual material (as described by state law) in a "patently offensive way," and as a whole the material does not offer "serious literary, artistic, political, or scientific value."

Hate Speech: Skokie, Illinois

The story of one of the most stunning examples of the doctrine of free speech taken to its logical extremes took place in the 1970s in the Chicago suburb of Skokie, Illinois. In this quiet, close-knit community of 69,000 people some 40,000 were Jews, many of whom fled war-torn Europe at the end of World War II in 1945. About seven thousand were survivors or families of victims of the Holocaust—the extermination of nearly six million Jews and imprisonment in concentration camps of many more—that took place in Nazi Germany during World War II (1939–1945). Skokie, Illinois, offered peace and solace to shattered lives that never would fully recover from the horrors of the Holocaust.

What Skokie residents saw as a threat to peace in their village began in the early 1970s when Frank Collin, the leader of a white supremacist group called the National Socialist (Nazi) Party of America, found his First Amendment rights to hold rallies and make speeches challenged by officials of Chicago's Marquette Park. A court case brought before the Seventh Circuit Court of Appeals was decided in Collin's favor in 1972, and he held rallies and made public speeches there unchallenged until 1976. In that year the park officials required a $250,000 bond from the Nazi group to cover policing costs. Collin objected, claiming harassment, and early in 1977 he wrote to surrounding suburban officials to state his intention to demonstrate in defense of his group's First Amendment rights.

In response, Skokie officials tried to block the protest. They set a $350,000 bond, obtained a county court injunction, and passed city ordinances designed to discourage Collin's group, including a ban on the use of military dress and the prohibition of the use of hate speech and distribution of hate symbols.

Collin engaged the help of the ACLU, which agreed that Skokie officials had violated Collin's First Amendment rights. He had a right to speak publicly, and his group had a right to gather for a rally. However, the Illinois Appellate Court refused to review the injunction, and the ACLU received heavy criticism for taking Collin's case. Some 50,000 people worldwide promised a potentially bloody counterdemonstration in the streets of Skokie.

Many members of the Skokie population were deeply offended by the case. To them, German Nazi leader Adolf Hitler, who masterminded the Holocaust, seemed to have risen from his grave to taunt them. Haunted by memories, they now felt forced to face their horror-filled past all over again.

Nonetheless, on the legal level, Federal Judge Bernard Decker ultimately sided with Collin and his group on the constitutional issues, striking down three of Skokie's city ordinances, paving the way for the Nazi demonstration on the steps of the Skokie city hall. The ACLU never wavered,

A Journalist Goes to Jail

How far does First Amendment protection reach? In July 2005, *New York Times* reporter Judith Miller was imprisoned for contempt when she refused a summons from a grand jury prosecutor to divulge her sources for a planned article-in fact, for an article she never wrote.

To some people—especially fellow journalists—Miller was heroic. She refused to cooperate with the summons despite the threat of jail because she had promised to shield her source and promised to protect anonymity in exchange for information. A seasoned, Pulitzer Prize-winning investigative journalist, Miller believed that to comply with the grand jury would be against the public interest in the long run. Miller and many other members of the press and public contend that in order to maintain freedom of the press, journalists must have the freedom to inquire and gather information freely—without interference from the government. If Carl Bernstein and Bob Woodward of *The Washington Post* had not been allowed to shield their anonymous source, the truth of the Nixon administration's involvement in the Watergate break-in of 1972 might never have been revealed. Forty-eight states and the District of Columbia have laws that shield journalistic sources in such cases, although there is no such law at the federal level.

However, at the federal level, precedence is not on Miller's side. In *Branzburg* v. *Hayes* (1972) the Supreme Court ruled in similar cases in which news reporters had been required to appear and testify before state or federal grand juries. The Court's decision held that these required testimonies in no way abridged the freedoms of speech and press guaranteed by the First Amendment. In 1978, the Supreme Court again held that it saw no such First Amendment right in such cases. In response to an appeal, the U.S. Supreme Court refused to review Miller's case. U.S. District Judge Thomas Hogan found her in civil contempt and sentenced her to as many as four months in jail. Some critics also denounced Miller for claiming rights for journalists that are not accorded other citizens.

Her defenders, meanwhile, invoke the American tradition of using civil disobedience to make a point and to stand up for a principle—as embraced by the Boston Tea Party, Henry David Thoreau, Rosa Parks, Martin Luther King, and many others.

holding that if First Amendment rights can be set aside for one group, they can be set aside for all. Deny free speech and assembly to a group of white supremacists today, and tomorrow it may be a group of Protestants or a group of Orthodox Jews, or a group of African-American school-teachers that is silenced.

In the end, the march was slated for Sunday, June 25, 1978. But Collin, meantime, had some political problems within his group, and on June 20 he called off the march. Few members of the group showed up on the appointed day, and they were greatly outnumbered. But it was the principle that mattered.

Picking up a theme from Milton's *Areopagitica*, Supreme Court Justice Oliver Wendell Holmes in 1919 wrote: "The best test of truth is the power of thought to get itself accepted in the competition of the market. . . . That at any rate is the theory of our Constitution." And he added: "We should be eternally vigilant against attempts to check the expression of ideas we loathe."

Unprotected Speech

Some types of speech are not covered by First Amendment protection. Here is a list of a few of them.

- Libel—printed statements that are both defamatory and untrue

- Slander—spoken statements that are both defamatory and untrue

- Fraudulent speech

- Fighting words—inflammatory speech that is both intended and likely to start a fight

- Obscene speech

- Personal threats

- Unwanted speech

Does Free Speech Enhance Democracy?

Many liberals favor a gag rule for vocal artists who have recorded songs that are politically incorrect to the point of being racist or inciting crime, or at the very least insulting. And many members of the political right see treason and sedition in the leftist antiwar rhetoric. Virtually everyone sooner or later wishes to restrict some speakers' rights to free speech. In fact, many people do not favor free speech for unpopular causes, even when no national emergency exists. In a survey conducted in the early 1980s, results showed very little support for free speech. Of the people surveyed, 71 percent thought atheists should not be allowed to set forth their views in a public auditorium; almost 60 percent thought the same rights should be denied to gay rights activists, as well as to anyone criticizing the government. Only 41 percent thought that people advocating "unpopular causes" should have the right to conduct mass protests.

But looking at the bigger picture—beyond the content of speech—freedom of speech operates as a pragmatic golden rule. If you want the right to express yourself, you must fight for the right of everyone to express himself or herself freely. Otherwise, the right disappears for everyone. As Kaminer points out, "This is, in part, a political strategy: Power shifts between your allies and opponents, often unpredictably. Your rights are most secure if they derive from established constitutional principles, not patronage. But the equal allocation of rights is also a moral imperative. I oppose censorship not simply because I fear the power to censor might be turned against the speech I like but in the belief that people have a moral right to indulge in speech I hate."

Pluses:

• Establishment of free speech for all is a successful political strategy for everyone— individuals who disagree with those in power as well as those who agree. Protected by constitutional principles, everyone's right to speak freely is more secure, thanks to a tit-for-tat agreement, not just patronage. As power shifts back and forth from group to group, free speech remains effective.

• Freedom of speech is the logical corner-stone of a free, democratic society. As Wendy Kaminer puts it: "Civil libertarianism doesn't rely on assumptions about our moral charac-ter. The belief that we should all enjoy the same rights doesn't reflect faith in everyone's ability or inclination to exercise rights virtu-ously. Instead, it's based on a conviction that we don't have to earn inalienable rights, or win them in a national popularity contest: Stupid, nasty people have the same right to vote as their intelligent, compassionate neigh-bors." And, as uncomfortable as that might make us feel sometimes, that equality makes sense in a society based on liberties.

• Allowing free speech adds to the market-place of ideas and keeps society involved in important issues.

Minuses:

• Freedom of speech gives license to assertions that may be untrue, injurious, or offensive.

• Persons speaking too freely could jeopard-ize—either knowingly or unknowingly—the security of our country.

Religious Freedoms and the Right to Assembly

The First Amendment's importance to free speech and a free press is so enormous that the rest of the First Amendment sometimes suffers neglect in people's minds. However, two highly important cornerstones in the bulwark of freedom and strong government are also covered by the First Amendment: religious freedoms and the right to freely gather in groups (the right to assembly).

A Wall of Separation?

On January 1, 1802, in response to an inquiry from the Baptist Association of Danbury, Connecticut, newly elected President Thomas Jefferson wrote a letter explaining his position on the federal celebration of religious holidays:

> **Believing with you that religion is a matter which lies solely between man & his god, that he owes account to none other for his faith or his worship, that the legitimate powers of government reach actions only, and not opinions, I contemplate with sovereign reverence**

that act of the whole American people which declared that their legislature should make no law respecting an establishment of religion, or prohibiting the free exercise thereof, thus building a wall of separation between church and state.

The First Amendment contains two clauses that some interpreters see as descriptive of a wall such as Jefferson described: First, it prohibits the government from establishing any religion (the Establishment Clause) and second, it supports freedom of religion (the Free Exercise Clause).

Before formation of the United States, nearly all the colonies had official churches with required attendance at Sunday services. The framers of the Constitution wanted to avoid the formation of a national church and especially wanted to keep the government from interfering with religion. And in *Cantwell v. Connecticut* in 1940, the Supreme Court ruled that no state could establish or create a religion.

By the same token, some interpreters of the Constitution see the wall working in the other direction as well, preventing religion from interfering with government and also allowing for diverse belief systems, including naturalistic, or nonmystical (or nonreligious), worldviews.

However, by no means does everyone agree that the two clauses in the First Amendment call for a "Wall of Separation" between church and all levels of government. Daniel L. Dreisbach, a professor of justice, law, and society at American University in Washington, D.C., and author of a book on this subject, argues that Jefferson was not referring to all government in his letter—only the federal government. He describes Jefferson's metaphor as "profoundly flawed," since it implies that the Constitution blocks the flow of influence from both directions, whereas the Constitution aims only to restrict the interference of the federal government in matters of religion, not vice versa. Dreisbach speaks for a large number of people who see "separation of church and state" as fundamentally different from the First Amendment precepts, which speak in terms of the nonestablishment and free exercise of religion.

Many people view their religious beliefs as essential to their identity and as necessary to moral and just action. Others favor a strictly cerebral and objective approach to just government. Moreover, in a nation with many different religious and cultural backgrounds, the Supreme Court has seen the need to foster respect for all in questions of religion, and the Court has made several decisions over the past sixty years that reflect that opinion.

The Supreme Court and Church/State Separation

The first case brought before the Supreme Court on the subject of educational policy with respect to separation of church and state was *Everson v. Board of Education* in 1947. In a major decision, the Court upheld a New Jersey statute that subsidized bus transportation for students attending parochial schools. Justice Hugo Black wrote the majority opinion, outlining a set of principles that set the legal precedent regarding the Establishment Clause. He wrote:

"The 'establishment of religion' clause means at least this:

- Neither a state nor the federal government can set up a church.

- Neither can pass laws that aid one religion, aid all religions, or prefer one religion over another.

- Neither can force nor influence a person to go to or remain away from church against his will or force him to profess a belief or disbelief in any religion.

• No person can be punished for entertaining or professing religious beliefs or disbeliefs, for church attendance or non-attendance.

• No tax in any amount, large or small, can be levied to support any religious activities or institutions, whatever they may be called, or whatever form they may adopt, to teach or practice religion.

• Neither a state nor the federal government can, openly or secretly, participate in the affairs of any religious organizations or groups and vice versa.

• In the words of Jefferson, the clause against establishment of religion by law was intended to erect 'a wall of separation between church and State.'"

He continued, explaining what a careful line he felt the Court must walk: "We must consider the New Jersey statute in accordance with the foregoing limitations imposed by the First Amendment." However, he explained, the Court had to uphold the state statute if it was constitutionally possible to do so—even though he considered that barely the case. He pointed out that the state of New Jersey could not remain consistent with the "establishment of religion" clause if it contributed "tax-raised funds to the support of an institution which teaches the tenets and faith of any church." But then there is the "free exercise" clause. "On the other hand," Black added, "other language of the amendment commands that New Jersey cannot hamper its citizens in the free exercise of their own religion. Consequently, it cannot exclude individual Catholics, Lutherans, Mohammedans, Baptists, Jews, Methodists, Non-believers, Presbyterians, or the members of any other faith, *because of their faith, or lack of it*, from receiving the benefits of public welfare legislation." Black wanted to be clear, too, on the implications of the First Amendment for a state providing transportation to public school children, adding that "we must be careful, in protecting the citizens of New Jersey against state-established churches, to be sure that we do not inadvertently prohibit New Jersey from extending its general state law benefits to all its citizens without regard to their religious belief." The Court's decision favored a broad interpretation of the Establishment Clause, as Black explained, but also adopted Thomas Jefferson's view that the Establishment Clause was intended to erect "a wall of separation between church and state."

Prayer in Public Schools

Before 1962, many classrooms across the country began each public school day with some form of "opening exercises" that included a short prayer either recited by the class or read by a class member or teacher. The day might begin with the Pledge of Allegiance to the flag, singing of a patriotic song such as "America," readings from the Bible, and the daily prayer. In many states the content of this routine might be left entirely or at least in part up to individual teachers, the principal, or the district school board. In New York State, the state Board of Regents sought uniformity and a demonstration of universal respect by writing a short "nondenominational" prayer to be used statewide. Intended to be positive but innocuous and inoffensive to members of all religions, the text of the prayer read: "Almighty God, we acknowledge our dependence upon Thee, and we beg Thy blessing upon us, our parents, our teachers and our Country."

A group of parents objected, however, characterizing the prayer as "contrary to the beliefs, religions, or religious practices of both themselves and their children." When the highest court of appeals in the state upheld the Board of Regents' prayer, the parents appealed to the Supreme Court. The Court reviewed the case, known as *Engel v. Vitale* (1962), which reversed the decision, striking down the use of prayers in public schools nationwide. Neither the fact that the prayer was nondenominational nor the fact that participation was voluntary kept the practice from being unconstitutional according to the Court. Specifically, Justice Hugo Black pointed out in his majority opinion that any prayer was a religious activity and that the state violated the Establishment Clause of the First Amendment by attempting to establish or encourage prayer. He described the prayer as "a solemn avowal of divine faith and supplication for the blessing of the Almighty," pointing out that everyone involved in the case, including the trial court, agreed that the prayer was religious. Justice Black also pointed out that many of the colonists who came to American shores seeking religious freedom had fled just this sort of government-approved program of prayer.

Engel v. Vitale was the first of a series of decisions by the Supreme Court that eliminated many religious activities from public functions, based on the Establishment Clause of the First Amendment.

Displaying Religious Symbols

Other issues surround the display of religious symbols in the public arena—for example in the rotunda of a state office building or on office walls or in court rooms—and these continue to be a hotly contested issue as this book goes to press. Given the directive of the Establishment Clause, should installation of religious symbols be allowed

A MONUMENT TO THE TEN COMMANDMENTS LOCATED IN THE ROTUNDA OF THE ALABAMA JUDICIAL BUILDING IN MONTGOMERY, ALABAMA, BECAME THE CENTER OF A SEPARATION-OF-CHURCH-AND-STATE CONTROVERSY. THE U.S. SUPREME COURT RULED THAT IT WAS A RELIGIOUS MONUMENT THAT HAD NO PLACE IN A FEDERAL JUDICIAL BUILDING AND INSTRUCTED SUPERIOR COURT JUSTICE ROY MOORE, WHO OWNED THE MONUMENT, TO TAKE IT DOWN ON AUGUST 27, 2003. MOORE REFUSED, WITH THE RESULT THAT HE WAS SUSPENDED FROM THE JUDICIAL REVIEW BOARD AND ULTIMATELY REMOVED FROM HIS POSITION FOR DISOBEYING A FEDERAL ORDER. THE MONUMENT WAS REMOVED FROM THE ALABAMA JUDICIAL BUILDING AND NOW RESIDES IN MOORE'S HOME CHURCH.

on public property? For example, should the Ten Commandments be displayed in government offices or be installed on the grounds of a state building? Should Christmas nativity scenes be allowed on school grounds? Should the phrase "God bless America" be displayed on public school signage?

Still more complex complications sometimes occur in interpretations when the two clauses overlap. For example, if a religious organization pays taxes, then the religion is supporting the state. Conversely, if the state gives a religion exemption from tax, then is the state supporting the church?

Several Supreme Court decisions relating to these questions come down on different sides, depending on the particulars of each case. For example, in 1990, in the case *Employment Division, Department of Human Resources of Oregon* v. *Smith*, the Supreme Court ruled that two American Indians were not entitled to unemployment compensation because they were fired for misconduct related to their use of peyote, an illegal drug—even though the drug was an element used in a religious ceremony of the Native American Church. In previous rulings, the Court had decided that a state could not make unemployment insurance available on the condition that an individual was willing to forego conduct required by his or her religion. But that was not the case here. Peyote was an illegal drug, regardless of who used it, and the Court ruled that the law had not singled out members of the Native American Church. The law's neutrality and general applicability protected it from this First Amendment challenge.

In *Jimmy Swaggart Ministries* v. *Board of Equalization of California* (1990) the Court found that the First Amendment did not protect a religious organization from paying sales tax (which applied generally to all retail sales) on the sale of religious materials. Another decision, *Board of Education of the Westside Community Schools* v. *Mergens* (1990), upheld the Equal Access Act of 1984 stipulating that public high schools had to allow student religious groups to use meeting-place facilities on the same basis as other extracurricular groups.

However, another case, from Florida, had the opposite outcome. In 1993 (*Church of Lukumi Babalu Aye* v. *City of Hialeah*), the Court disallowed a Hialeah, Florida, municipal ordinance against animal sacrifice. The Court deemed the law to be unjustly aimed at a practice of the Santería religion.

All of these decisions show the Court's recognition of a

need for equal treatment of individuals even if some state-religion separation may be compromised.

Should Church and State Be Kept Separate?

Pluses:

• In an ethnically diverse society such as the United States, freedom of religion is especially important, and the best way to maintain it is by ensuring that the government establishes no religion and that all citizens have the freedom to exercise their religion.

• As the Connecticut Baptists put it in 1803, religious matters should be "distinct" from the state so as to keep religion unmarred by secular matters, and to keep clear that matters of conscience belonged to God's realm, not the government's.

• Parents who are not religious or whose religious beliefs are not in the majority in their school district do not have to worry about what religious beliefs are being taught to their children in public school.

• When government and religion work too closely together, corruption may result due to conflicts of interest. With separation, less corruption is likely.

Minuses:

• Many people think that a good society requires the moral influence of religion, and therefore a government that relies on the moral influence of religion will be stronger and more beneficent.

• Separation of church and state may prevent children who attend public school from learning important religious precepts alongside school curriculum.

• Existence of a national religion might give the nation a sense of unity of purpose and encourage a common worldview.

• Some experts, such as Dreisbach and historian Philip Hamburger, contend that separation of church and state is a misinterpretation of the constitution.

Freedom of Assembly

When people gather in groups they can wield tremendous power, and, additionally, sometimes property is damaged, transportation and traffic are blocked, and people may get hurt. Consequently, in times of emergency, when more control either is necessary or appears to be so, freedom of assembly may be the first civil liberty to be affected. Civil libertarians therefore see a special need for watchfulness in this arena, as with all First Amendment rights.

In June 2003 the city of Sacramento, California, faced a typical challenge. A large and controversial convention was coming to town, the Ministerial Conference and Expo on Agricultural Science and Technology. Presentations were expected to be made on genetic engineering and its uses in agriculture and food production, and several groups with agendas ranging from radical to conservative were poised to launch demonstrations to gain attention for their differing points of view.

The City Council decided to pass an emergency ordinance, which called for tight controls and restrictions on who could demonstrate and what they could bring. Looking back, Mayor Heather Fargo recalls, "When we first passed this ordinance, I think it made some sense, we had a lot of information that was very troubling and of great concern to the City Council." Afterward, some critics thought they had overdone it, banning bandanas, baseball bats, or signs having "lengths of lumber" with a width greater than two inches. The regulations, they later discovered, would have barred veterans or ROTC groups if any of their members carried weapons.

Later, no longer faced with such an intense, high-profile event, the City Council found they did not want to let go of some of the restrictions. In an early draft of a revised ordinance, they allowed weapons if they were unloaded and inspected before a parade or gathering. One plan called for having police inspect them, marking them if acceptable. However, they had outlawed spontaneous gatherings of more than seventy-five people, and they had banned glass containers as a safety hazard. The revised ordinance met with heavy criticism from marines, activists, civil rights attorneys, and others. "You're taking otherwise legal items and making it illegal if they choose to express the rights of free speech," said civil rights attorney Jeffrey Schwarzschild. "It's unenforceable, untenable and unconstitutional."

Some members of the council remained cautious, especially considering post-9/11 concerns about terrorism and some of the city's experiences with the agricultural conference. "I wouldn't want to be in a parade or a march with [people carrying] weapons that were brought here," remarked City Councilwoman Bonnie Pannell. Others pointed out that, given the likelihood that protestors might vandalize property, become violent, or masquerade as terrorists, a measure of caution was called for. Because of the continuing acts of terrorism worldwide, the risks created by gather-

ings, both impromptu and planned, are causing considerable thought at every level.

The Right to Gather in Groups

In good times and bad, people frequently need to gather in
groups to make a point to others (protests and demonstrations); to discuss problems, programs, pressures, and
many other topics of mutual concern and interest; or to
enjoy recreation.

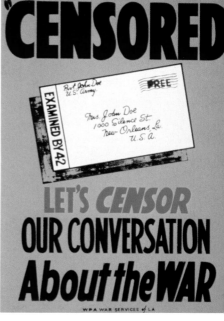

POLICE ARREST A PROTESTOR DURING A
DEMONSTRATION OF CIVIL DISOBEDIENCE
IN SAN FRANCISCO, MARCH 14, 2003,
WHEN ABOUT A HUNDRED ACTIVISTS
PROTESTING THE WAR IN IRAQ BLOCKED
AN INTERSECTION AND CLOSED DOWN
THE CITY'S FINANCIAL DISTRICT.

DURING WARTIME AND OTHER NATIONAL
EMERGENCIES, CENSORSHIP—ESPECIALLY
SELF-CENSORSHIP—FREQUENTLY APPEARS TO
BE IN THE NATION'S INTEREST. YET, SOME PE
PLE ASK, WHAT ARE WE PROTECTING, IF NOT
FREEDOM? THE BALANCE BETWEEN SECURITY
AND FREEDOM IS CONSTANTLY ADJUSTING.

On the other hand, groups of any type can become unwieldy, out of control, even dangerous, and they can endanger themselves as well as the safety, property, and lives of others. What if someone does have a gun? What if police brought in to keep the peace find themselves surrounded by an angry crowd? Wouldn't it be simpler just to ban gatherings of people?

Pluses:

• Freedom of assembly is an important right. Without it, we can lose common avenues of protest, the freedom to gather in churches, town meetings, and even simple, celebratory parades.

• Gathering together is natural, and is one of the best ways to protect our freedoms against encroachment.

Minuses:

• Crowds can shift quickly and become dangerous and violent, especially when emotions run high.

• Noise, garbage, and traffic blockage create nuisance factors that interfere with the privacy of nearby residents and have an economic impact on businesses in the vicinity.

The Right to Bear Arms

"A well regulated Militia, being necessary to the security of a free State, the right of the people to keep and bear Arms, shall not be infringed."

—The Second Amendment

Much controversy exists about the meaning of the Second Amendment. Does the Second Amendment grant to individuals an absolute right to own guns? Does it mean that no restrictions by the government are allowed? The language is not clear. Historians point out that in the early years of independence, the government had to rely on a civilian militia, an ad hoc group of soldiers that could be called forth from their homes as they were needed. So they always had to have a gun at hand.

Today, we no longer rely on a militia for our only protection. Gun control advocates contend that the amendment refers only to weapons used by a state militia or a national guard.

The Supreme Court has had no enthusiasm for the argument brought to the table by gun owners. In a 1939 case the Court pronounced that "[i]n reality, the Second Amendment applies only to firearm ownership in the context of a 'well-regulated militia,' and not individuals" (*United States v. Miller*, 1939). In the *Miller* case the Court reviewed the transport of a sawed-off shotgun across state lines, ruling that such a weapon would not be useful to a state militia and therefore the Second Amendment established no right for an individual to bear and use such a weapon.

Now, the wind seems to be shifting. In *United States* v. *Emerson* in 2001 the Fifth Circuit Court of Appeals ruled:

> **We have found no historical evidence that the Second Amendment was intended to convey militia power to the states . . . or applies only to members of a select militia. . . . All of the evidence indicates that the Second Amendment, like other parts of the Bill of Rights, applies to and protects individual Americans. We find that the history of the Second Amendment reinforces the plain meaning of its text, namely that it protects individual Americans in their right to keep and bear arms whether or not they are a member of a select militia or performing active military service or training.**

Self-Defense and Hunting

The point has been made many times that people are at a distinct disadvantage if the military and police are armed but individuals are not. Advocates further argue that, in both urban and rural settings, many people feel safer if they have a gun for protection. Congress voted in September 2004 to dismantle gun control laws in the District of Columbia, where owning a gun has been illegal since the 1970s. From the House floor, Rep. John N. Hostettler of Indiana made the following remark: "It seems to me that a criminal's dream would be a city where law-abiding citizens are disarmed. Preventing these law-abiding citizens, our fellow Americans, of Washington, D.C. from enjoying the same protections the rest of us enjoy is unfair and unsafe."

Finally, many people in rural areas use their guns for hunting, either for sport or for food, and a long tradition supports this activity, particularly in the Western states. Gun advocates also raise another question: Should the government have the right to restrict the use of guns and require gun owners to register weapons that they have in their possession?

Columbine and Other Tragedies

On the other side, many people point out that every year dozens of hunting accidents occur. They also cite the tragic deaths, either accidental or due to anger, that have occurred because a gun was too close at hand. Equally tragic are the attacks on children in schoolyards, or by students on their classmates, as in the case of the Columbine High School massacre. (However, people also say that if all teens or teachers were armed, schoolyards and classrooms would

AN APRIL 20, 1999, SECURITY VIDEOTAPE VIEW OF ERIC HARRIS (LEFT) AND DYLAN KLEBOLD IN THE COLUMBINE HIGH SCHOOL STUDENT CAFETERIA. IN A VIOLENT ATTACK THAT ENDED WITH THEIR SUICIDE, THE TWO BOYS GUNNED DOWN AND KILLED A TEACHER AND TWELVE FELLOW STUDENTS.

no longer go undefended and tragedies like Columbine would come to an end.)

Should Guns Be Controlled?

Gun control safety regulations include such measures as a waiting period when buying a gun, gun registration, background checks, restrictions on certain types of guns, such as semiautomatics, and efforts to minimize the use of guns in anger. Are such controls needed? And are they constitutional? Or is gun control an infringement of individual rights?

Pluses:

• Gun control advocates generally interpret the Second Amendment as a provision for an armed state militia composed of individuals who would therefore need to have weapons on hand in case they were called by the government to fight for their state and their country. Since national and state-level defense are no longer provided for in this way, they reason, individuals no longer have the need to be armed that the Second Amendment addresses. This viewpoint bears out the longstanding interpretation of the U.S. Supreme Court handed down in the 1939 case *U.S.* v. *Miller* that the individual's right to bear arms revolves around its usefulness to a state militia. An interpretation by the Sixth Circuit Court in *U.S.* v. *Warin* in 1976 is even more restrictive: "Since the Second Amendment . . . applies only to the right of the State to maintain a militia and not to the individual's right to bear arms, there can be no serious claim to any express constitutional right to possess a firearm." (This opinion does seem to deviate from the language of the Second Amendment.) Either line of reasoning offers gun control advocates reinforcement for their position that at least some measures of gun control are in keeping with the Bill of Rights.

• To keep guns out of the hands of irresponsible individuals, gun controls—such as registration, waiting periods, and background checks at purchase points coupled with restriction on the types of guns that can be owned—can reduce the number of crimes or accidents that happen as a result of a passing moment of anger or frustration.

• If safety training were required with gun ownership, some gun-related accidents might be averted.

• Child-safety locks on handguns would eliminate a cause of many tragic injuries and deaths.

Minuses:

• Owning a gun enables people to take care of themselves.

• The presence of a gun in a household can deter burglaries.

• Owning a gun, especially one to be used for hunting, is part of an American tradition.

• Requirements for training, registration, and waiting periods are all unnecessary regulation by the government, as are restrictions on the type of gun one is allowed to own.

• Mandatory child-safety locks on guns add an unnecessary expense for people who have no children and do not allow children to have access to their guns.

• Gun control does not address the problem of gun ownership by criminals and irresponsible individuals. People abusing the right to bear arms frequently obtain guns illegally through the black market. Thus gun control cannot always "control" those who most need it and instead limits the legitimate use of guns by responsible people.

6

The Right to Privacy

What we think of today as the right to privacy began as the Fourth Amendment, "the right of the people to be secure in their persons, houses, papers, and effects, against unreasonable searches and seizures. . . ." Roughly, it means, "I shall remain in control of my records and shall decide who sees them, and I shall remain in charge and in possession of what is mine—from physical property to information about my own person—unless there is some compelling reason otherwise and then only with an explicitly stated search warrant."

The right to privacy does not have to do with being free to act dishonestly in secret (as some critics may state or imply). Instead, it is about remaining in control of one's choices, one's assets, and one's finances.

Today, technology has changed much of the specifics about retaining one's right to privacy. Giant, centralized commercial databases compile details about our every move, from shopping habits and preferences to financial and credit data to travel patterns to medical records. Electronic trails enable Web-page owners to track our movements on the Internet, tracing the Web sites we visit, the information we supply, and the purchases we make. In a world where all this is possible,

AFTER SERVING A SEARCH WARRANT ON MARCH 20, 2002, U.S. CUS-
TOMS AGENTS CARRY BOXES FOR COLLECTING EVIDENCE AT AN OFFICE SITE
IN HERNDON, VIRGINIA. THIS SEARCH WAS PART OF A TWO-STATE RAID OF
FIFTEEN LOCATIONS IN VIRGINIA AND GEORGIA THOUGHT TO BE CONNECTED
WITH THE FUNDING OF TERRORISM.

of course, governments have begun to think in terms of making law enforcement more effective and efficient through the
use of similar giant databases. Whereas even felons were once
able to leave one state and settle in another with impunity
(sometimes allowing a repeat of their earlier crimes), that
loophole has now been replaced by interstate database sharing. The FBI has always maintained a huge database, but
many patterns were lost to analysis because indexing and
cross-referencing was not always complete. Many of these
glitches have been modified, and with a few quick keystrokes
a match-up for a modus operandi (a recognizable pattern or
method of operation) may pop up across state lines.

Searches and Seizures

In Chapter 1 we discussed in some detail the provisions of
the USA Patriot Act, which allowed investigators access to
library and bookstore records to review what types of
information a suspect is reading. Similarly, agents could, in
the course of an investigation, set up surveillance on a
library computer used by a suspect.

Secret Surveillance and Investigations

A 1998 survey by the New York Civil Liberties Union found at least 2,380 surveillance cameras monitoring public places in New York City; an estimated 2,000 of them were private. The phenomenon is not limited to the Big Apple. The Carmichael, California, branch of the Bank of America is typical, with a row of eight cameras along the back wall, trained on every area of the bank. Of course, the main purpose of cameras in most commercial businesses is to reduce "shrinkage" and theft, or to identify the thief in the hope of recouping losses and punishing shoplifters. Placing a camera at a high-profile potential terrorist target, such as an airport or the U.S. Capitol Building, is one thing, but a blanket surveillance with central watchpoints covering schools, shopping malls, and city streets is invasive, according to representatives of the American Civil Liberties Union (ACLU, a national organization that advocates the protection of individual rights through litigation, lobbying for legislation, and educational programs).

Surveillance Cameras— Good or Bad?

Pluses:

UCLA law professor Eugene Volokh, writing for the *Wall Street Journal*, says that camera systems can promote both security and liberty.

• Volokh points out that a camera positioned in a public place (not the ones in dressing rooms) can only see what is plain to see—what any passerby would see—and therefore he does not consider it invasive.

• Cameras are a tool that can be used appropriately or dishonestly. They provide a degree of power to those providing the surveillance.

• Cameras may deter some criminals.

• Volokh admits that the cameras open the door to abuses. Using face recognition software, keeping the images indefinitely by failing to recycle the tapes, and creating a pool of data would all be dangerous misuse. However, barring that kind of misuse, surveillance cameras are really just useful, effective tools for law enforcement.

Minuses:

The ACLU says there are four reasons surveillance cameras do more harm than good:

• Cops are much more effective than cameras. Big crimes such as the terrorist attack on the World Trade Center towers would probably never be detected with cameras. They actually are only good at catching smaller-scale crimes, such as shoplifting.

• Cameras don't generally stop crime, they just displace it—causing the crime to be committed someplace that is not on video, such as a change of venue for a drug deal.

• A powerful surveillance system is an invitation for abuse. For example, videos can be used by employees to blackmail clients, if clients commit indiscretions on camera.

• Once put in place, they won't go away; in fact they will expand, and what once may have been a tolerable exposure may become out of control; most people not starring in a reality-television show would prefer to have some off-camera moments.

More on Privacy

Generally, privacy has become a big issue in America. Businesses try to assure customers that they will not share information about those who do business with them. Some laws, such as medical confidentiality laws, are designed to protect a patient's privacy. Meanwhile several laws in existence or under consideration, such as Megan's Law, offer public access to information for protecting against such social threats as child sexual abuse, communicative diseases such as AIDS, and terrorism. National ID cards may help control terrorism and illegal immigrants. But some people ask, are the costs to individual privacy greater than the gain? Identity theft—the almost complete loss of control over one's personal and financial information—has become a rapidly mushrooming crime, ruining the financial credibility of many innocent victims.

Medical Record Confidentiality Laws

Does a woman or man about to be married have a legal right to know that Huntington's chorea runs in the family into which she or he is about to marry—and that it may strike the couple's children as well? Does a potential employer have the right to know prior to hiring that an applicant has a debilitating disease such as fibromyalgia or multiple sclerosis?

Not long ago, many people worried about other people having access to their medical records without their permission. Without seeking his patient's permission, a doctor might talk to a man's daughter about a heart problem he didn't want her to worry about. Medical researchers might access records without knowledge or permission. Today, much stronger standards are in force since the Department of Health and Human Services (HHS) established standards for the privacy of individually identifiable health information. The rules apply to health plans, health care clearinghouses, and certain health care providers. According to the preamble of the HHS standards document that went into effect in February 2001, "These protections will begin to address growing public concerns that advances in electronic technology and evolution in the health care industry are resulting, or may result, in a substantial erosion of the privacy surrounding individually identifiable health information maintained by health care providers, health plans and their administrative contractors." The objectives include a respect for privacy and the "personal life," a cessation of uncontrolled profiteering at patients' expense, and the establishment of patients' rights to disclose their personal affairs to whom they want and when, where, and under what circumstances they want.

This respectful stance has its downside, however, as indicated by some of the questions above. Jill Schramm, staff writer for the *Minot* [North Dakota] *Daily News* tells the story of a woman who has struggled for more than seven years to obtain release of information about her father's suicide so that others might avoid such a tragedy in similar circumstances. Consumer advocate groups oppose changing the law in ways that make inroads on the patient protections of confidentiality and self-determination. When the man's daughter finally saw the records, she found out that during more than three weeks of hospitalization he had decided to discontinue his medicine and talked often of suicide. However, the doctor, respectful of the father's privacy, told the daughter on his release simply that he was doing well. Although the hospital had taken precautions against suicide during his stay, the daughter was not told to be watchful, and she was not made aware of his frame of mind or unmedicated condition.

There appear to be no easy answers.

Megan's Law

Seven-year-old Megan Kanka was a girl from New Jersey who was raped and killed by a known child molester who moved in across the street from her family without their knowledge. Megan's Law was conceived to prevent future tragedies of this kind. It provides for sex offender registration and community notification of a registered sex offender's presence. The federal legislation was signed by President Bill Clinton on May 17, 1996, and by 2005 nearly all states were offering state-sponsored Internet access to public listings that locate registered sex offenders—providing knowledge and awareness to potential victims. In California, Megan's Law was passed by the state legislature in August 2004 and was signed into law by the governor a month later. Today, anyone can access the information on the Web site: www.meganslaw.ca.gov/homepage.htm. It can be searched by name, address, city, zip code, county, park, or school.

Few people would criticize this breakthrough measure, which helps protect innocent children and other potential targets from becoming victims of a heinous crime. However, the Web site administrators point out, "Extreme care must be taken in the use of information because mistaken identification may occur when relying solely upon name, age and address to identify individuals." More than one person in the same city or county may have the same name—and an innocent person could be confused with a registered offender. Moreover, although the law provides a fine for harassment using the Megan's Law information, the accessibility of the information can result in invasions of privacy for individuals and their families—invasions not intended by lawmakers.

National ID Cards

The issue of national ID cards was still undecided in spring 2005, although Congress seems more and more serious about establishing this tool for identifying an individual. This is not a new idea. Citizens of many countries in Europe, Asia, and South America are required to carry a national ID card. However, several countries have rejected the idea, including Australia and New Zealand, which share the English common law tradition with the United States.

Congress recently endorsed electronically readable drivers' licenses, standardized from state to state, which in many ways is a giant step toward a national ID card. The electronic age has made further features possible, including a fully searchable, coordinated national database and cards containing embedded radio frequency identification (RFID) chips. The U.S. State Department already plans to begin issuing passports soon that use the RFID technology. Other possibilities include retinal scans, fingerprints, DNA data, and RFID tracking technology.

Proponents of the national ID card see the establishment of a nationwide database and electronic identification system as necessary to defeat the infiltration of terrorists and illegal immigrants into the country. As F. James Sensenbrenner, Republican representative from Wisconsin, remarks, "American citizens have the right to know who is in their country, that people are who they say the are, and that the name on the driver's license is the real holder's name, not some alias."

Those who object see the establishment of national ID cards as both a financial burden on the states (which would be expected to administer the program) and as a loss of power to the Department of Homeland Security (which would have full authority to design state ID cards and drivers' licenses). In the past, racial, political, and religious discrimination have often served as motivations for national ID cards. Pakistan uses ID cards to enforce a quota system, while in the Netherlands they are used to reduce border controls. In any case, at the root of the system is an increase in police power—the ability to demand the ID card under penalty of detention.

In May 2005, Congress passed draft legislation (assumed likely to pass) requiring all fifty states and other U.S. jurisdictions that issue drivers' licenses to verify that all applicants for a new license or renewal reside here legally. Those against the law say that it will amount to a national ID card; those in favor say it will help to deter terrorism.

Identity Theft

When someone steals your identity and represents himself or herself as you, that person has committed a crime known as identity theft (ID theft) or identity fraud. The U.S. Department of Justice's Web site on ID theft says the terms apply "to all types of crime in which someone wrongfully obtains and uses another person's personal data in some way that involves fraud or deception, typically for economic gain."

Many details of your ID can be obtained relatively easily by criminals and used to impersonate you—withdrawing funds from your bank account, opening credit accounts in your name and charging on them, using credit accounts you have already opened, and making other transactions. People in the street can "shoulder surf," walking close to you to observe security codes and account numbers you may punch in at an ATM or to overhear you give your Social Security number or credit card number over the telephone. They may raid your trash or use "Dumpster diving" to gain information about you. Fraud also takes place through deceptive e-mails (for example, e-mails claiming to represent your bank and "phishing" for your account information by asking you to "update" their files) or through phone calls.

One especially ambitious criminal ran up $100,000 in debt on a stolen credit card, bought real estate (with a federal home loan) and motorcycles, and even purchased handguns in his victim's name. In addition to the damage to his reputation, the victim and his wife ended up paying $15,000 of their own money to repair the damage—a project that took them four years. Since identity fraud was not a crime at the time, the perpetrator got off with a light sentence (for making a false statement to purchase a firearm). He never made restitution to the victim for any portion of his crime.

In 1998 Congress established identity theft as a crime, and a veritable arsenal of phone numbers, contacts, and advice is now available to stop ID thieves before they get started.

An Equitable and Changing Balance

For every thing there is a season,
and a time for every purpose under heaven:
A time to be born, And a time to die;
A time to plant, And a time to pluck up that which is planted;
A time to kill, And a time to heal;
A time to break down, And a time to build up;
A time to weep, And a time to laugh;
A time to mourn, And a time to dance;
A time to cast away stones, And a time to gather stones together;
A time to embrace, And a time to refrain from embracing;
A time to get, And a time to lose;
A time to keep, And a time to cast away;
A time to rend, And a time to sew;
A time to keep silence, And a time to speak;
A time to love, And a time to hate;
A time of war, And a time of peace.
—Ecclesiastes (Chapter 3, Verses 1 through 8)

This book began with the idea that we must look to the sum of human experience and wisdom for guidance in resolving the difficult controversies that stem from the challenges of trying to live together in peace. The many valid objections, clashes, disagreements, and debates raise the bar high. Civil liberties experts advise that we must find a balance point, and we must be prepared to adjust that balance point as the need arises.

Not everyone agrees with the quote from *Ecclesiastes* at the beginning of this chapter. There are those who believe that there is never a time for war or a time for hate, for example. But history teaches that much truth can be found in these fifteen short verses. Things change. People rightfully point out that the American Constitution is now over two hundred years old. Perhaps we do not need to carry guns in the same way our seventeenth- and eighteenth-century predecessors did. Or perhaps we have need

CUSTOMS AGENTS AND AN ILLEGAL IMMIGRANT. SINCE 9/11, ILLEGAL IMMIGRANTS HAVE BEEN UNDER MUCH MORE SCRUTINY THAN IN THE PAST, AND ARE FAR MORE FREQUENTLY DEPORTED.

of self-defense now more than ever. Today we have communication through Internet Web sites and e-mail and cell phones—methods unthought of two hundred years ago. Should the rules for civil liberties be different? Or does it really matter whether ideas are carried via pony express or electrons? As the French proverb says, "Plus ça change, plus c'est la même chose." ("The more things change, the more they are the same.")

What rules and guidelines can we use to be sure of fairness? How can we ensure justice and an equitable coexistence? How can we be certain that we have struck the right balance? How can we be sure that we have not made our nation and the world less safe by allowing so much freedom?

No one really knows definitive answers to these questions. But knowledge and freedom of information are probably two of our greatest allies. The more we know about other cultures and other communities, the better we can live side by side with differences. We can know what to expect and with knowledge we may find mutual respect and self-knowledge as well.

Furthermore, for the democratic process to function, every citizen needs to know how our system of government works. Admittedly, recognizing when to stand firm and when to compromise is difficult and complicated.

Where, exactly, does our right to privacy begin and end? When people are arrested, what rights should they have? If someone is imprisoned, what rights should that person have? How important is the right to own a gun to the survival of democracy? Does a pregnant woman have a right to an abortion? Should one have the right to end one's life? Is contraception a right? How about the right to marry the person you choose? Are violent video games protected forms of speech? Does the right to be free of "cruel and unusual punishment" preclude the death penalty or the torture of suspected terrorists?

Reaching a consensus on a list of fundamental rights is

only the foundation. The real work begins with the clashes that take place over conflicting rights. A woman may have a First Amendment right to protest abortion outside the local clinic, yes, but what does that do to the right to privacy for the patients who go there for help?

As Wendy Kaminer writes:

> **Civil liberties often conflict with civil rights, as liberty inevitably conflicts with equality, dividing liberal and conservative libertarians. The 1964 Civil Rights Act that prohibited discrimination in public accommodation and transit systems (as well as in the workplace) subordinated the associational freedom of white supremacists to the equality rights of African Americans. The conflict between the freedom to discriminate and the right to equal treatment in public places was properly resolved about one hundred years too late, most Americans would probably agree. But it's worth noting that the conflict existed. Today, while laws against official segregation are no longer controversial, workplace regulations aimed at benefiting women, racial minorities, or other historically disadvantaged groups, like disabled people, raise similar questions about balancing employers' liberties with employees' rights.**

The complexities are as varied and numerous as the people of our country, for everyone is in some way unique—and we seek to live together with as much freedom, strength, individualism, and mutual respect as we can. And at the same time we seek to live as safely and securely as possible.

Notes

Introduction
p. 9, "to strike the United States and its allies": Associated Press, "Bin Laden Admits Ordering 9/11," *Chicago Sun Times*. www.suntimes.com/ooutut/terror/binladen30.html (accessed December 1, 2004).

Chapter 1
p. 12, "... goaded the White House ...": Jesse Jackson, "Military Tribunals Threaten Civil Liberties," *The Terrorist Attack on America*, Mary E. Williams, ed. San Diego, CA: Greenhaven Press, 2003, p. 106.

p. 14, "I had supposed ..." Roger B. Taney, quoted by Alan M. Dershowitz, *Shouting Fire: Civil Liberties in a Turbulent Age*. Boston: Little, Brown, 2002, p. 420.

p. 19, "aid the terrorists": "Ashcroft Denounces Court Rulings," *Washington Post*, November 13, 2004. Reprinted by the *Chicago Tribune*, November 13, 2004, p. 10.

p. 20, "While we did not find ...": U.S. Department of Justice Office of the Inspector General. Report to Congress on Implementation of Section 1001 of the USA Patriot Act. www.fas.org/irp/agency/doj/oig/patriot0904.pdf (accessed March 13, 2005).

p. 21, "The federal government needs to explain ...": Masci, David, and Patrick Marshall. "Civil Liberties in Wartime," *CQ Researcher*, December 14, 2001. Reprinted in Williams, *The Terrorist Attack on America*, p. 99.

p. 21, "We make no apologies ...": Shannon McCaffrey, "Report: Sept. 11 Dragnet 'Harsh': Justice Department Defends Detentions."

San Jose Mercury (CA) *News*, June 3, 2003, Page 1A.

p. 21, "The Constitution": Patrick Leahy quoted by Masci and Marshall, p. 97.

p. 21, "Our efforts have been crafted . . .": "Excerpts from Attorney General's Testimony Before Senate Judiciary Committee," *The New York Times*, November 7, 2001. www.albany.edu/mumford/wtc/ashcroft.htm (accessed April 29, 2005).

p. 25, Ashcroft "tried to assure lawyers . . ." Associated Press, "Ashcroft Defends Patriot Act to Lawyers' Society," *Sacramento Bee*, November 16, 2004, p. A17.

p. 25, "specifically tailored . . .": Bob Barr, "Patriot Act Games: It Can Happen Here," *The American Spectator*, August 19, 2003. conservative.org/columnists/barr/030819bb.asp (accessed September 2, 2003).

p. 26, "The real way . . .": Barr, "Patriot Act Games."

p. 27, "What would happen . . .": Jonathan Turley, "Connecting the Dots to Save Our Freedoms," *The Sacramento Bee*, January 6, 2003, p. B5.

p. 30, "In general Americans . . .": James D. Torr, ed. *Homeland Security*. At Issue: Opposing Viewpoints Series. San Diego, CA: Greenhaven Press, 2004, p. 10.

p. 31, "connected the dots": Former FBI agent David Major, cited by James D. Torr, *Homeland Security*, p. 10.

p. 33, "We have been using . . . ": Michelle Madigan, "Report Card on the Patriot Act: Government Cites Successes, While Privacy Watchdogs Say Failures and Problems Aren't Publicized." PC World.com, October 9, 2002. www.pcworld .com/resource/printable/article/0,aid,105786,00.asp (accessed December 21, 2002).

pp. 33–34, "raises privacy . . . ": Lee Tien, quoted by Madigan.

p. 35, "aggressive detention . . .": Masci and Marshall, *Civil Liberties in Wartime*, p. 99.

p. 37, "If the new tools . . . ": Senator Dianne Feinstein in "Statement of Senator Dianne Feinstein at a Hearing Examining Effectiveness of USA Patriot Act and Border Security Legislation on War on Terror," October 9, 2002. News from Senator Dianne Feinstein of California. feinstein.senate.gov/Releases02/4-borderoversightp.htm (accessed April 29, 2005).

p. 37, "a crucial weapon . . .": Associated Press, "ACLU, Arab Groups Challenge Patriot Act," *The New York Times*. July 30, 2003. www.nytimes.com/aponline/national/

AP-Patriot Act-Lawsuit.html?pagewanted=print&position= (accessed July 30, 2003).

p. 37, "the worldwide terrorist threat . . .": Knowlton.

p. 38, The Terrorist Screening Center . . . : White House Homeland Security Web page, December 11, 2004. www.whitehouse.gov/homeland/ (accessed December 11, 2004).

pp. 38–39, "This legislation has...": In his 2003 State of the Union: White House Homeland Security Web page, December 11, 2004. www.whitehouse.gov/homeland/ (accessed December 11, 2004).

p. 39, One of Benjamin Franklin's . . .: Franklin, Benjamin, *Historical Review of Pennsylvania*, 1759, reprinted in John Bartlett, *Familiar Quotations*, Bartleby.com, 2000, 10th Edition. www.bartleby.com/br/100.html (accessed November 17, 2004).

pp. 39–40, Widespread, deep concern . . .: ACLU (List of Communities That Have Passed Resolutions, August 31, 2004. www.aclu.org/SafeandFree/SafeandFree.cfm?ID=11294&c=207 (accessed November 28, 2004).

p. 40, Critics disparage . . .: Associated Press, "ACLU, Arab Groups Challenge Patriot Act."

p. 41, "America faces a crucial test . . .": Strossen, Nadine, Timothy H. Edgar, et al. "ACLU Testimony at a Hearing on 'Security and Liberty' Before the National Commission on Terrorist Attacks Upon the United States." December 8, 2003. www.aclu.org/SafeandFree/SafeandFree.cfm?ID=14589&c=206 (accessed December 6, 2004).

Chapter 2

pp. 44–45, "one very simple principle. That principle is . . . ": John Stuart Mill, *The Subjection of Women* (Philadelphia, Lippincott, 1869), quoted by Alan M. Dershowitz, *Shouting Fire: Civil Liberties in a Turbulent Age*. Boston: Little, Brown, 2002, p. 121.

p. 48, "The first claimed external source . . .": Dershowitz, *Shouting Fire* p. 9.

p. 48, "Nature has no goal . . .": Baruch Spinoza, *Ethics I* (1677), quoted by Dershowitz, *Shouting Fire*, p. 11.

p. 49, ". . . rights must be discovered . . .": Ronald Dworkin, *Taking Rights Seriously*, Cambridge, MA: Harvard University Press, 1977, p.81.

p. 49, "the best political program . . .": op.cit., p. 177.

pp. 60–61, "Civil libertarianism is a nonpartisan . . .": Wendy Kaminer, *Free for All: Defending Liberty in America Today.* Boston: Beacon Press, 2002. p. xii.

p. 62, "To his supporters, . . .": "Civil Rights," *1953 Collier's Yearbook*, Microsoft Encarta Reference Library, 2005.

p. 66, "Left and right . . .": Kaminer, *Free for All*, p. xvi.

Chapter 3

p. 70, "Evil manners . . .": John Milton, *Areopagitica. A Speech for the Liberty of Unlicensed Printing to the Parliament of England.* www.gutenberg.org/etext/608 (accessed December 11, 2004).

p. 72, "miserable savages, . . .": Emery, Edwin, *The Press and America: An Interpretive History of the Mass Media.* Englewood Cliffs, NJ: Prentice Hall, 1972, p. 28. Quoted by Elaine Pascoe, *Freedom of Expression: The Right to Speak Out in America.* Issue and Debate. Brookfield, CT: Millbrook Press, 1992, p. 19.

p. 72, "any Glut . . .": Emery, *The Press and America*, p. 20.

p. 73, "The liberty of the press . . .": U.S. Constitution: First Amendment. Annotations p. 6, Freedom of Expression: Speech and Press. supreme.lp.findlaw.com/constitution/amendment01/06.html (accessed December 6, 2004).

p. 73, "The Zenger trial is . . .": Linder, Douglas, "The Zenger Trial: An Account," 2001. Famous American Trials: John Peter Zenger Trial, 1735. www.law.umkc.edu/faculty/projects/ftrials/zenger/zenger.html (accessed December 6, 2004).

pp. 76–77, "[T]he sheriff was deaf . . .": Ibid.

p. 77, "The loss of liberty . . .": Ibid.

p. 79, "The question before the Court . . .": Ibid.

p. 80, "The trial of Zenger in 1735 . . .": Ibid.

pp. 83–84, "Public assemblies and public speech . . .": William Orville Douglas, quoted by Linder in "*Feiner* v. *New York.*" www.law.umkc.edu/faculty/projects/ftrials/conlaw/feiner.html (accessed December 13, 2004).

p. 92, "The best test of truth . . . ": Supreme Court Justice Oliver Wendell Holmes, dissenting opinion in *Abrams et al.* v. *The United States.*

p. 93, Of the people surveyed . . .: Kaminer, *Free for All*, p. 17.

p. 93, "This is, in part . . .": Ibid., p. xiii.

p. 94, "Civil libertarianism . . .": Ibid.

Chapter 4

pp. 95–96, "Believing with you . . . ": Thomas Jefferson, quoted by Daniel L. Dreisbach, "How Thomas Jefferson's 'Wall of Separation' Redefined Church-State Law and Policy," *Chronicles*, May 2003, www.chroniclesmagazine.org/Chronicles/May2003/0503Dreisbach.html (accessed March 11, 2005).

p. 96, "profoundly flawed": Ibid.

pp. 97–99, "The 'establishment of religion' clause means . . .": *Everson* v. *Board of Education*. www.law.umkc.edu/faculty/projects/ftrials/conlaw/everson.html (accessed December 13, 2004).

p. 100, "contrary to the beliefs . . .": Introduction to *Engel* v. *Vitale*. sinfo.state.gov/usa/infousa/facts/democrac/47.htm (accessed March 11, 2005).

p. 103, "distinct,": Alan Wolfe, "Church and State Should Be Separate." *Civil Liberties*, Auriana Ojeda, ed. Opposing Viewpoints. San Diego, CA: Greenhaven Press, 2004, p. 77.

p. 104, "Some experts . . .": Philip Hamburger, author of *Separation of Church and State*, as described by Wolfe, *Civil Liberties*, pp. 76–77.

p. 105, The City Council . . .: Terri Hardy, "Council Repeals Parade Rules: Ordinance Drafted at a Time When the City Feared Violent Protests 'No Longer Seems to Fit' The Mayor Says," *Sacramento Bee*, December 1, 2004, pp. B1–B3.

Chapter 5

p. 111, "Since the Second Amendment . . .": "Gun Control: Why Doesn't the ACLU Support an Individual's Unlimited Right to Keep and Bear Arms?" ACLU Library Web Site. archive.aclu.org/library/aaguns.html. (accessed November 15, 2004).

Chapter 6

p. 116, A 1998 survey . . .: Kaminer, *Free for All: Defending Liberty in America Today*, Boston: Beacon Press, p. 26.

Chapter 7

p. 127, "Civil liberties often conflict . . ." : Kaminer, *Free for All: Defending Liberty in America Today*, Boston: Beacon Press, p. xv.

Further Information

For Further Reading

Darmer, M. Katherine B., Robert M. Baird, and Stuart E. Rosenbaum, eds. *Civil Liberties vs. National Security in a Post–9/11 World*. Amherst, NY: Prometheus Books, 2004.

Hatamiya, Leslie T. *Righting a Wrong: Japanese Americans and the Passage of the Civil Liberties Act of 1988*. Palo Alto, CA: Stanford University Press, 1993.

Isler, Claudia. *The Right to Free Speech*. Individual Rights and Civic Responsibility. New York: The Rosen Publishing Group, 2001.

Nardo, Don. *The Bill of Rights*. Opposing Viewpoints Digests. San Diego, CA: Greenhaven Press, 1998.

Neier, Aryeh. *Defending My Enemy: American Nazis, the Skokie Case, and the Risks of Freedom*. New York: Dutton, 1979.

Williams, Mary E., ed. *The Terrorist Attack on America*. Current Controversies. San Diego, CA: Greenhaven Press, 2003.

Web Sites

American Civil Liberties Union (ACLU)
www.aclu.org

This site reflects the concerns of the ACLU, which sees itself as "our nation's guardian of liberty." Nearly everyone disagrees (or at least feels uncomfortable) with the ACLU at some time because the group focuses on correct process, not "correct" ideas. They seek to protect the guarantees offered by the First Amendment: equal protection under the law regardless of race, sex, religion, or national origin; fair treatment by the government whenever loss of your liberty or property is at stake; and your right to privacy.

Cato Institute
www.cato.org

The home site of the Cato Institute, a nonprofit research organization headquartered in Washington, D.C., and dedicated to individual liberty, limited government, free markets, and peace. Founded in 1977, the Cato Institute's name derives from *Cato's Letters*, a series of newspaper articles written under the pseudonym "Cato" by John Trenchard and Thomas Gordon and published from 1720 to 1723. These essays helped found the philosophy upon which the U.S. government was originally built.

EverGreen USA Patriot Act
www.evergreen.edu/library/govdocs/hotopics/usapatriotact/

Primary sources and other materials concerning the USA Patriot Act, including a presentation on "The USA Patriot Act and Intellectual Freedom." This site is sponsored by the Evergreen State College Library, Olympia, Washington.

GovExec.com - Homeland Security
www.govexec.com/homeland

News and analysis for government professionals, including articles and columns from the print magazine, *Government Executive*, providing an inside look at government priorities.

The Homeland Security link provides breaking news about domestic security issues.

Homeland Security Institute (HSI)
www.homelandsecurity.org/

Headquartered in Sherlington, Virginia, this federally funded research and development center was established by Analytic Services, Inc. (ANSER), under the direction of the Department of Homeland Security (DHS) of the U.S. government. According to the Web site, "The HSI will assist the Department in formulating and addressing important homeland security issues, particularly those involving policy and security where scientific, technical and analytical expertise is required." ANSER was established by the Rand Corporation in 1958, with ties to the federal military and intelligence communities. The HSI home page supplies a "Threat Level" gauge, links to HSI's newsletter and journal, and topics of interest to the general public.

National Coalition Against Censorship (NCAC)
www.ncac.org

More than thirty years old, this organization focuses on threats to freedom of speech, or freedom of expression, including book censorship, threats to the free flow of information, obscenity laws, creationism, attacks on school textbooks, and more. Two special projects focus on arts advocacy and sex and censorship.

National Rifle Association (NRA)
www.nra.org

A source for news, books, pamphlets, materials, and information relating to firearms, the right to bear arms, gun safety, target shooting, hunting, and surrounding issues and topics.

U.S. Department of Justice: Preserving Life and Liberty
www.lifeandliberty.gov/

The official Department of Justice site for the USA Patriot Act, with many useful links, including major speeches about the

Patriot Act, a Patriot Act field report, and a page entitled "Dispelling the Myths."

U.S. Supreme Court
www.supremecourtus.gov

Contains a wealth of information about the U.S. Supreme Court, its history, biographies of current justices, content of oral arguments, information about past cases, opinions, the docket of cases showing status of cases for both the current and prior term, search capabilities, and other related information.

The White House: Homeland Security
www.whitehouse.gov/homeland/

Offers news releases and information from the White House for the general public regarding homeland security.

Bibliography

Brown, Cynthia, ed. *Lost Liberties: Ashcroft and the Assault on Personal Freedom*. New York: New Press, 2003.

Darmer, M. Katherine B., Robert M. Baird, and Stuart E. Rosenbaum, eds. *Civil Liberties vs. National Security in a Post–9/11 World*. Amherst, NY: Prometheus Books, 2004.

Dershowitz, Alan M. *Shouting Fire: Civil Liberties in a Turbulent Age*. Boston: Little, Brown, 2002.

Dreisbach, Daniel L. *Thomas Jefferson and the Wall of Separation Between Church and State*. New York: New York University Press, 2003.

Friedman, Lawrence M. *American Law in the 20th Century*. New Haven, CT: Yale University Press, 2002.

Lieberman, Joseph I. "No Excuse for Second-Class Justice," *Washington Post National Weekly Edition*, January 7–13, 2002, reprinted as "Military Tribunals Need Not Erode Civil Liberties" in *The Terrorist Attack on America*, Mary E. Williams, ed. San Diego, CA: Greenhaven Press, 2003.

Masci, David, and Patrick Marshall. "Civil Liberties in Wartime," *CQ Researcher*, December 14, 2001. Reprinted in *The Terrorist Attack on America*, Mary E. Williams, ed. San Diego, CA: Greenhaven Press, Inc., 2003.

Neely, Mark E. Jr. *The Fate of Liberty: Abraham Lincoln and Civil Liberties.* New York: Oxford University Press, 1991.

Pascoe, Elaine. *Freedom of Expression: The Right to Speak Out in America.* Issue and Debate. Brookfield, CT: The Millbrook Press, 1992.

Torr, James D., ed. *Homeland Security.* At Issue: Opposing Viewpoints Series. San Diego, CA: Greenhaven Press, 2004.

Walker, Samuel. *Civil Liberties in America.* Contemporary World Issues. Santa Barbara, CA: ABC-CLIO, 2004.

Will, George. *With a Happy Eye But . . . : America and the World, 1997–2002.* New York: Free Press, 2002.

Index

Page numbers in **boldface** are illustrations.

About the Authors

Ray Spangenburg and Kit Moser have coauthored more than fifty books and one hundred articles for children and adults on science, technology, critical thinking, and social issues. Their most recent book for Marshall Cavendish Benchmark, *Genetic Engineering*, in our Open for Debate series, was named a Notable Social Studies Trade Book for Young People in 2005. They are also coauthors of a five-volume history of science and the award-winning biography *Niels Bohr: Gentle Genius of Denmark*.